ITCHING TO LOVE

Beloved NPR Storyteller Shares Her View of Dogs,
Men, Motherhood, Lasagna, and the Founding Fathers

ITCHING TO
LOVE

the story of a dog

Award-Winning Author

SHELLEY FRASER MICKLE

Published by Forefront Books, Nashville, Tennessee.
Distributed by Simon & Schuster.

Library of Congress Control Number: 2024921453

Print ISBN: 978-1-637633-39-7
E-book ISBN: 978-1-637633-40-3

Cover Design by Mary Susan Oleson, Blu Design Concepts
Interior Design by Mary Susan Oleson, Blu Design Concepts
Cover Illustration by Carrie Tillis

Printed in the United States of America

"Twenty seconds of laughter is the equivalent in exercise of three minutes of strenuous rowing.

—NORMAN COUSINS
Head First: The Biology of Hope and the Healing Power of the Human Spirit

*For all the mothers
in the world*

CONTENTS

Warning—

Nothing in this tale will move forward in a straight line. Since we tend not to see life while we are living it, this will be a zigzagging story from when I put it through the sieve of memory to let fat slices of illumination separate out.

It all began when I started telling stories on my local NPR station. One day, I got a call from NPR's *Morning Edition* in Washington, DC, asking me to tell my stories nationally. And I did so for the next six years. Since this one would not fit into three minutes of broadcast time, I'm writing it down here. Winding my memoir around a dog seemed a good way to begin to answer: "What did he see in me that I could not see in myself?"

It took years, though, to come to an understanding.

—Shelley Mickle
FEBRUARY 2025

It seems to me that many of us, especially me, find that it's much easier to give love than to receive it.

CHAPTER ONE

The Buddy Problem

The neighborhood had meetings about him. He lay in the street as a speed bump. Was he trying to commit suicide? If so, none of us wanted to oblige him. Driving up the hill at night on a country road with no street lights, our cars lit him up as a wad of wrinkles, just in time to swerve or stop. Some said lying there he looked as if someone had dropped their trousers and run off.

Everyone knew his name.

The meetings ended in a whimper because nobody really knew the right thing to do with him. No one wanted to call the dog police on him. Or on his owner. Theirs was a pitiful story.

He had a feed bowl, always full. He was under flea control and worm management. His nails were clipped. Nothing on him smelled too bad. But every day as soon as his owner went to work, he dug out from under the fence and spent the day stealing from farm to farm.

One neighbor whined: "He took my sweater."

Another threw in: "He knows when I've gone for groceries. When I took one bag into the house, he stole toothpaste out of another."

Soon our imaginations bloomed as if we were concocting a Mark Twain tall tale. "He ran off with my beer. He came back, though, sober and with his teeth still stained by garbage."

"I found a ham wrapper under my car!"

"I saw my ugly plaid coat hanging off an azalea bush."

"So, you got it back?"

"No. I'm actually glad he stole it."

You see, Buddy often left a trail of his pilfered goods on his way back to where he knew his food bowl was. Then he'd take up his self-assigned job as a speed bump, lying in the middle of our road.

At one time or another—in childhood, at least—we all seem to get the idea we don't belong in the same family with those our birth certificate says we are eternally related to. Buddy was a year old at the time. With seven years of a dog's life equal to one of ours, Buddy was similar to a second-grade kid with genetic angst. His home did not fit him.

And he was not pretty.

His coat was the brown color of an old man's liver spots. His chest and feet were white. His toes had brown dots like a bird dog had dived in the gene pool. His head was as wide as a gallon pickle jar and sported a forehead like that of a Labrador retriever. But his jaws hinted of bulldog, the scary kind, and his eyes were snake-yellow with pink rims. Often he looked as if he had tied one on. From the rear, he had the muscular hips of a Rottweiler. Most endearingly, his booty hole was outlined by the most perfect caramel-colored butterfly. But most people missed seeing that birthmark and assumed he was like that Johnny Cash song about tough men who might kill you just to watch you die. Buddy was often the victim of profiling. Everyone who met him backed up.

No one—not even faculty vets with oodles of degrees—ever could identify all the breeds that had gone into his whopper-sized body. It was clear: Buddy's mama belonged to a long line of loose women.

Buddy was proof of our yet undeveloped region. In North Central Florida where we live, there are enough rural parts that dogs can spoon in the woods unchaperoned. Natural springs here are clear enough that you can stand in the water and see your toes. Miles of untamed woods mix hardwood hammocks with pine forests as if they have a real-estate agreement to coexist in peace. Parts are as untouched as when men tromped through looking for eternal youth. And mistletoe and moss hang on tree limbs as if they haven't yet heard that every day is not a holiday. Buddy was a Florida brown dog. He was an outlaw in the outskirts.

* * *

The first time I saw Buddy was about a year after I moved onto our street. There were several of us married couples who built houses on large acreages because we wives were horse nuts and wanted to take care of our horses ourselves rather than board them. There's something quite wonderful about lying in bed in the dark and hearing your beloved horse chomping grass outside your window. My neighbors across the street, the husband of whom looked like Hopalong Cassidy from my childhood, had built a house and barn on ten acres. Hoppy's young wife, who resembled Dolly Parton, was as horse crazy as I was. She displayed two palominos in her pasture, and then talked Hoppy into taking her to the world Quarter Horse show. She wanted to see what *that* was all about.

They drove off in October. She did not come back. If she ran off with a cowboy, I didn't ask. It seemed insensitive to fish for an answer. Each day Hoppy went to work and came back to that big brick house with two palominos in the pasture and sat in a yard chair looking hang-head sad and scary lost. Just before sunset, he'd climb up onto the tallest palomino, of whom he was terrified, and ride white-knuckled down the road as though he hoped honing his riding skills might bring his young wife back. He'd then sit out under two oaks until dark as if going inside the house would echo with former okay times and reek of unbearable loss.

A few weeks later, a strange car appeared in his drive. My phone rang not long after that.

"Shelley, I just want you to know. . ."

Hoppy sounded like a B-flat on a bassoon—sad, sad, sad. "There's no hanky-panky going on over here. I want you to know that. I've just rented out a room."

"Good," I said. "And remember, I'm always here if you need anything."

Only too well did I know how an empty house can sound. My kids had grown up and moved out. And my husband plays golf. No more needs to be said.

Hoppy let a room to a young female vet student who soon acquired a puppy. I saw that puppy only at a distance from across the road. He looked like a mudball bouncing at her feet. She obviously loved him, at least for the moment. She gave him the most common name for a dog: Buddy. She also found him to be good homework. She clipped off his breeding parts. She gave him shots and cleaned his teeth. She bought him a blue collar. But she was a young thing and could not stay in any one place too long.

With no warning, she was gone.

Buddy sat in the yard—fat, wormed, bathed, and in a funk.

The first day he dug out, he headed down the street to watch my neighbor who was breeding Labrador retrievers. Buddy crept under her fence and studied how she threw tennis balls for her dogs who gleefully retrieved them. Buddy didn't give a hoot about bringing a ball back to anybody. He didn't give a fat hello, either, about hunting or pointing at birds. Fowl and man-sports left him cold. Armadillos could get him a little worked up, and occasionally he'd run one down and crack its shell with his bulldog jaws like it was a Brazil nut. But rarely did he even get his knickers in that much of a twist. Mostly he lay like a lump, drunk with family-envy.

As the neighborhood began meeting about him, the retriever breeder stood up and demanded, "Somebody's got to confront Buddy's owner about his dog irresponsibility."

"OK." And we nominated her.

"No, I think it should be a committee." She amended our motion.

We named the committee. We called it the Buddy Problem. No one wanted to head it, much less be on it. Hoppy just couldn't take our criticism, we feared. One more thing and he might sink into nothingness like a popped balloon. His life was already leaking. We hoped one day to look over and see that he and Buddy had punched through their funk and discovered each other. They'd be romping in the yard like in a movie scene—happy music playing—no dialogue, just violins and harps.

Sometimes at sunset I saw Buddy go up to Hoppy in his yard chair and put his pickle-jar-sized head on Hoppy's knee. And Hoppy's hand would rest woodenly between Buddy's floppy ears.

After the morning following a recent neighborhood meeting, I was leaning over, cleaning out my own horse's hooves on a crystal-blue afternoon, when I spied Buddy behind me. He was sitting at the edge of the barn. His yellow eyes looked like chickpeas. I have to admit he was a good bit scary-looking. I was a little disconcerted. After all, I was aware I was on his food chain.

But I've never been afraid of a dog. I'm also not the kind of woman to scold a dog that is not mine. I felt no right to discipline him or teach him any manners. He was Hoppy's, and I was going to respect that.

I lifted my horse's other front foot and went at the clumped manure with my hoof pick. Bending down, I was now facing Buddy where he sat in the doorway still staring at me. "Go home," I said. He looked deeply into my eyes, and I swear it seemed I could hear him saying, *Here's looking at you, kid.*

He then bolted under my horse's belly, grabbed one of my horse's galloping boots in his mouth, and took off. That pair had cost me $62.99. Not even yelling a word that a sailor would use had any effect on Buddy. I chased him across the road. "Hey you, that's mine!" I even gave out a Rebel yell that Shelby Foote would be proud of. But he was by now far into Hoppy's yard.

Hoppy always conveniently left up the garage door about a foot for Buddy to get to his food bowl and out of bad weather. When Buddy shimmied on his big stomach under it, I reached for the door handle to push the door the rest of the way up. Daylight lit up Buddy sitting stone still in the corner. In his mouth was my horse's galloping boot. While looking at me as if to say *Sorry*, he spit it out. It fell beside what I saw was my denim shirt that I'd left in the barn days earlier. There was also my comb. A sock. A towel with my wiped sweat on it, along with two pieces of mail that must have fallen out of my recycling bin—a plea for money from a local Democrat and from a Freedom Caucus Republican. They were all lined up as if Buddy had taken a home economics course.

In many decades of living, I've discovered a strange truth. It's one that brings an unexpected twist to this business of living. It seems to me that many of us, especially me, find that it's much easier to give love than to receive it. In seeing how Buddy hoarded parts of me, I was given a new view of my identity. In his own way, Buddy was telling me he held me in high regard, collecting parts of my life in an exhibit worthy of a national museum of art.

Oh, for Pete's sake! Let's call it what it was. He was displaying the inexplicable, otherworldly, never-die kind of what we can't seem to ever get enough of—*love,* even if it was of the canine kind. And he was giving it to me with no strings attached except my willingness to receive it.

It had taken me nearly forty years to get ready for Buddy.

In my long past, I've had a few really weird boyfriends, but I've never had the obsessive adoration that Buddy was offering me. It was then that I began the search for why Buddy had chosen *me* to leap the barrier between canine and *Homo sapiens* to form an unbreakable bond.

I loved him fiercely in the way a person does before having children, which in itself deepens one's capacity for love by the measure of the depth of the ocean.

CHAPTER TWO

Bad Poetry

I've always loved dogs. They are up there on my list with horses, cats, kids, cheesecake, and good men. But I was never allowed to have a dog in my childhood. I was always told they cost too much. Their needs, you know: they have to have food and a fence and worming, and insurance in case they bite anyone. Free dogs were OK because the strays I brought home were the traveling kind. They never stayed long. And as for a horse, which I was obsessed with having, too, my father had the most rigid rule: *never buy anything that eats while you're asleep.*

He was an engineer who had lived through the Great Depression and World War II rationing. He squeezed every nickel until the eagle screamed. He taught me over the years to be super thrifty, to watch my money. He even put a speed bump in our driveway so we wouldn't have to use the brakes more than necessary when coming home, thus saving them from wearing out before their time had come. We'd bump up over that blob of concrete, cut the engine, and coast to the front step.

Maybe in that vein, I began to save money by writing really bad poetry to give as gifts on holidays and birthdays. I tell everyone that I write it bad on purpose because it makes it funnier. But the truth is, it's the best I can do. And it's free.

Poems about dogs became my favorite, maybe because I can't look at a dog's face without bursting out in laughter—not in a sweet, dainty, girlish laugh, but in the beer-belly, let-'er-rip kind of guffaw of a redneck. It's the sound owned by men I grew up with, are related to, and love.

* * *

"We heard of a dog in Duluth
Who was told he was uncouth.
So he signed up for lessons
At Miss Scarlett's etiquette concession
And got a job in a kissing booth.

∽

A dog fell in love with a pony
He didn't think it was gauche or tony
But when he got the shaft, he only laughed
And sued for palimony.

∽

I heard of a dog in Indianola
Who fell in love with a woman named Lola.
He quickly gave her up
When she taught him to sit up
And beg for Coca-Cola.

∽

There once was a dog hooked on caffeine
When he lived in Abilene.
But he moved to a place called Hope
And took up smoking dope.
Now he's clean, living in Bowling Green.

∽

He should have been named Elvis or Sting

Prince or Bing

Because Buddy was way too ordinary

For a dog so hunky-dory.

And it was no big deal when his

Behind grew to the size of a hog's end-zone

Because he didn't give a hoot

About the size of his patoot.

He just wanted someone to own.

* * *

My husband was training to become a brain surgeon in Boston when he came home one night and put a puppy in my lap. I named the dog Brumble because I liked the sound. He was half German shepherd and something else his mama didn't want to talk about. But she had dressed him cool in all black with a perfect white tip on his tail.

We were in our twenties then—my husband and I. We were learning about love and about being far away from home. We didn't know anything about the end of life except what my husband knew from ushering patients to the doorstep of their last day when they could no longer be saved. And then ten years later, Brumble brought the experience of death home, teaching me about grief. Big dogs don't tend to live much longer than that.

He'd helped us through eight years of neuro-surgical training, a stint in the military, two moves across country, and the birth of two children. I loved him fiercely in the way a person does before having children, which in itself deepens one's capacity for love by the measure of the depth of the ocean. We left him buried in our snow-covered backyard in Nebraska after my husband decided to take a job at the University of Florida as the one and only pediatric neurosurgeon. We had a hunger for warm weather and the South where we had grown up.

Twenty years later, I stood on a hilltop on the outskirts of this college city and paged my husband. Only three times before in all those hectic years had

I done that—paged him, asking the hospital operator to find him. And each time it had been after I'd crashed the car so I could warn him before he came home to see that the car now had a rumpled fender and a bashed-in hood. I'd learned that while I hemmed and hawed leading up to the bad news, he'd interrupt and impatiently say, "Would you hurry up? I've got my hands in somebody's brain." That was always the best time to tell him bad news.

This time, though, it was joy I could not contain. "I've found it."

"What?"

"Our farm—at least our farm-to-be."

"Where?"

"Only about fifteen miles out."

In New England, we'd vowed to live on a farm one day. We had fallen in love with the beauty of the region and those gentlemen farms around Concord and Lincoln. But the Florida countryside had not yet spoken to us. Besides, we found raising kids was easier close to town where we could cut down on hauling them to this and that.

Now, all that was past. The kids were grown and gone. And despite my father's warning never to buy anything that eats while I'm asleep, I had. I'd bought a horse and was now the owner of two of them, Skip and Robert Redford. With the ache of an empty nest, I'd revived an old childhood passion. I was becoming a cowgirl, even if it was at the last minute.

"I'll come out and look at it as soon as I finish up in the OR. Stay there. By the way, where is *there*?"

I gave him directions and waited. Finding a hilltop in Florida is about as common as being born naturally blond. And this hilltop was spectacular. Soon after five p.m. my husband—a Roy Rogers lookalike—drove up in the red pickup we'd bought to pull boats and horse trailers. Together my husband and I stood on the hill made of clay and looked out over the twenty acres that sloped to a sinkhole that was surrounded by woods. We had to have it, and I took down the phone number for the Realtor whose sign was stuck in the ground.

Across the road, Hoppy had already broken ground.

"Building's a pain in the ass," my husband pointed out after we got home. "Everybody who's done it always says don't do it."

"Yes, but we've never before much minded pain." It was true. We were proud of having done a respectable number of foolhardy things in our twenty-six years of marriage. Building a farm seemed less of one.

I called the Realtor and asked him to meet me on the land. The next day, while my husband was waging war against brain tumors, I went alone to stand on the hilltop again and wait for the guy with the facts. He drove up in a swell car and got out and lumbered up the slope to meet me. His smiling face was as circular as a skillet, and instantly

I liked him and knew he'd be game for a loopy story. "I'm looking for a place to build a farm and retire a horse," I explained.

He grinned and opened his notebook. "Oh, I love horses. Raised my kids on one. What you got?"

Few pleasures to a horse owner can equal talking about what's out in the barn. At the time, my horses were being boarded, but I was on the trail of having my own barn. "A Quarter Horse I bought five years ago," I said, trying to be brief and polite. "That's when my first child went to college. But now the horse is getting old. He can no longer sweat— his sweat glands are just all used up. I've tried that old cowboy remedy of giving him beer so he'd sweat out the alcohol, but more often than not it doesn't work. And it also made me feel like when I rode him I was his designated driver."

He laughed, thank goodness. So I went on. "Now I want to build him a barn with an overhead fan. I promised him I'd keep him forever. I think it's a privilege to care for one until the end."

"What color is he?"

"Flea-bitten gray. But he doesn't have fleas." I jabbered on while he handed me a piece of paper with the land's specs on it. "When I was little," I explained, "I wished for a prince on a white horse, but to tell you the truth, I really wasn't all that interested in the prince. It was his horse I wanted. And now I have one. In fact, I guess I've got them both, the horse and the prince. And the horse is *particularly* handsome. But that's not his strong point."

"What is?"

"Honesty. Will put up with anybody without taking advantage of what they don't know. We used to put my daughter's boyfriends on him. If the horse didn't trot, we knew the boyfriend was unbalanced."

He cut his eye at me and chuckled.

"Skip takes care of everyone," I added.

"Skip? Skip what? Is he registered?"

"Yep," I said with pride. "I tried to take out

insurance on him but the adjuster said he wasn't worth the premium. He *is* registered, though. Skip 'n Bailey. Bailey was his father."

"Lord have mercy and give me a trust fund!" the Realtor bellowed. "I raised six kids on that horse. Bought him when he was three. He must be what—fifteen now?"

"Seventeen," I said, "and he's got a trick back. It goes out every once in a while and I have to call the chiropractor." I was quickly digesting the news that this Realtor had once owned my beloved horse, which was not only a shock but also a sweet coincidence. Being my father's daughter who hated to part with every dime, I was even wondering if this could mean a better deal for me.

The Realtor lifted his chin and smiled. He could smell a sale coming, but he also cared, I could tell, about how his life had now circled with mine. "Well, these twenty acres will make the best place in the world for Skip to retire. And if you want to make an offer, I'll see that it goes through. When can I see Skip?"

In twenty-four hours it was a done deal. I tore a page out of *Southern Living* with a floor plan on it and took it to a reputable builder. "Do it," I said. "Only move that wall a little here, and that one a little there. And oh, yeah, we want a barn attached to the house with overhead fans in the stalls. And also in the house, hardwood floors because my dog's got a little pee problem."

By then we were on our third decade of dogs—a *real* German shepherd this time, imported and purchased. We'd wanted a babysitter for our teenagers, though she never could stop their parties when we left town.

I'd made a terrible error in naming her. After we picked her out as a puppy and took her home, I did not realize she would grow up to be beautiful and daunting and clearly of megawatt breeding from parents named Count Something-or-other and Fräulein Too-De-Sweet. I gave her a whore's name by mistake—Boom Boom. But then, I've had a long history of being dumb about those sorts of things. My worst example of that naiveté was when I was in college and heard a guy yell over to his friend, "What's the word, Turd?" I thought that was the most perfect rhyme I'd ever heard. I took it on as my own, casually calling out to my sorority sisters, "What's the word, Turd?" until one kindly took me aside and told me the definition that I was ignorant of. Even today, I grieve for the loss of that crisp, perfect rhyme.

Every few days, with Boom Boom beside me, I visited the house going up. We spent most of our time admiring the barn.

I had found the land in November, and by the next October, we were moving in. I sat on our farmhouse porch with Boom Boom beside me. "Living room, kitchen. Master bedroom, garage." Bossing the movers gave little pleasure.

Other times I'd maneuvered around moving day with two young children underfoot. And while I sat, I pulled up those memories. Those moves with young children had meant that picnic sandwiches had been pre-made. Card games kept them out of the movers' hair. The move from Nebraska to Florida had especially stayed stored in my memory like barbecued beans that'd never lost their tang. My son had been two then and had overheard one of the movers say "damn." Once he learned saying that word was a no-no, he, like every two-year-old is prone to do, picked up the mover's vocabulary with the precision of a Xerox machine. "Damn table," he said as they loaded it into the van. "Damn desk. Damn bed. Damn chair."

While I sat on moving day on our new farmhouse porch, it was a damn pitiful quiet time. Boom Boom, who had a dog disease that was causing her to lose the use of her legs, lay by my side. I paid the movers and waved them goodbye. Boom Boom pulled herself up and wobbled behind me into my new household, both of us feeling palpably strange without a kid underfoot.

We had our farm. We had our dream. But it was just not right. The kids were gone. The dog was nearly dead. And we'd never gone long without either. The impending loss was like a chasm we were about to fall into.

If you're prone to think mystically in any way, you might want to say Buddy fell into my life from heaven. But nix that thought; he smelled too bad for that.

. . . laughter is our survival mechanism.

CHAPTER THREE

Stella, Buddy, and Fred

I hadn't been in our new farmhouse long when it became uncomfortably clear that we'd have to let Boom Boom go. She dragged herself from house to barn. She lay in the house on the new hardwood floors and more often than not soiled them. It was painful to watch and heartbreaking to accept that her quality of life was no longer worth her effort.

We put her to sleep ourselves—my husband with the drugs, and me holding her after I took her for a drive while she gnawed a T-bone steak in the back seat. We buried her under a pine tree on our dream-come-true farm.

Not long could I manage without the sight of something standing up and wiggling at the sight of me. I simply couldn't be without a dog. The cats were fine—the two we'd had for over a decade. But you know how cats are. They keep you guessing. If they love you, they don't often let it show.

My horse vet noticed my down-in-the-mouth mood. I mean, I was dripping grief over Boom Boom like a tree shedding leaves in a windstorm.

"I have a dog I need to get rid of," he said, then qualified the sentence in appropriate adverbs. "She's sinking emotionally. You see, I named her Stella because I thought it would be hilariously cool to go outside and scream 'Stella!' like Marlon Brando in *A Streetcar Named Desire*. But she got hit by a car, broke her pelvis, and because I'm a vet I knew I would have to keep her in a cage for three months to let her heal, if she ever really did. So I did. She's OK now, but I don't want her living with my five other dogs that pick on her. She's more than sad. I think she's getting suicidal."

Well, what more did I need to hear?

I drove over to get her. On the way home,

she cowered in the back seat like a female convict headed to death row. Little did she know she was being taken to paradise.

I had named our farm Blueberry Hill Farm after that Fats Domino song, "I Found My Thrill on Blueberry Hill." And now Stella was part of that thrill.

She was a purebred Doberman with devil ears, fixed and pointed for perpetuity, and solid black with an uncanny ability to lift her lip above her teeth in an imitation of a human smile. True to human nature, most people read her grin as a snarl. But I knew she was just channeling Teddy Roosevelt with his famous grin depicted in cartoons as a glowing row of white teeth.

She caused me to have many visits from the dog police because all my neighbors were afraid of her, or rather, uneasy with her when she wandered onto their property. Because, well, I'm an utter failure as a dog owner. I think of my dogs as my friends who don't need leashes. I use a leash only when I take them to the vet for a heartworm test. And when I rode Skip on our twenty acres and in our neighborhood, I wanted Stella with me, following along, running unrestrained, wallowing in her freedom. It was fun, playing cowgirl. It was just us—a girl, her horse, and her dog, hours together swimming in nature with the feel of being in a temple, kneeling to a higher power.

And then came Buddy. Sure, he may have started visiting every day because of Stella. As dogs, they'd had their breeding parts snipped away, but that never gets in the way of a true friendship. It wasn't until I discovered all those pieces of my life lined up in Hoppy's garage that I realized and accepted my special responsibility. *I* was who Buddy had to be near. It was *me* he called home. Always, he needed to look into my eyes and connect. He would watch me, studying my every motion and mood. I was his world, and I was happy to be it, realizing I treasured his adoration as naturally as my first morning sip of coffee—total bliss.

Now it was Buddy, Stella, and Skip that became the daily triumvirate gracing my world. Those moments seeped into my writing muscle. The desire to write had struck me early, the aspiration to inspire a good feeling, maybe even a belly laugh, in a reader.

The human is the only animal that laughs, except the hyena, whose laugh is actually akin to a human karate yell. The fact that the human laugh is considered a reflex suggests that it has a protective function like a cough, a sneeze, or an eyeblink, ridding us of something potentially harmful that has crept in.

As a reflex, when we laugh the sound comes bellowing out; we simply can't help it. That's why in a place where laughing is taboo, such as at a wake, it can become irrepressible as it did when one of my friends unconsciously commented, "It sure is deadly quiet in here." That was all it took. Our laughter spread from one to the other through our clamped lips as if a match had been struck over a pile of dry cornhusks. We were rude but certainly distracted from realizing that one day we'd each be lying in a box with others looking at us. (Which has led me to design my own headstone that will say either *This heat is killing me* or *It was all a dream*. I've thought about asking everyone to stand over my grave while singing "Row, Row, Row Your Boat," but the prospect of all that singing out of tune seems an insult to Eliphalet Oram Lyte, the composer, who really does have one of the great names in the English language.)

Back in the days of the Greeks, philosophers studied comedy and came up with three theories to explain why we laugh.[1] Aristotle decided we laugh when we feel superior, which explains slapstick and the pie-in-the-face gag. Freud got in the act, saying we laugh when we break rules or say something considered taboo. This explains why letting go a blue streak of cusswords can elicit a hearty laugh if not a titter. And why the character of Sophia in *The Golden Girls* could say outrageous things and be forgiven since she'd had a stroke, which caused her social filter to become out of whack.

Best of all, the incongruity theory explains wordplay, wit, and irony, a higher form of comedy meant to tame death wishes or murderous impulses, meaning that when two things come in the mind that are not always associated, an explosion of delight bursts out. My favorite example of this is when Oscar Wilde, in the Tower of London for some sex crime, sent a note to the queen telling her that if this was the way she treated her prisoners, she didn't deserve to have any. Since Oscar was well known as a homosexual, often being put in the slammer for some indiscretion, his comment was loaded all the more.

It's pretty obvious now that I've come to my

point: laughter is our survival mechanism.

Thanks to neuroscience, we now know that a laugh sets off a flood of chemicals known as endorphins. Thank God for chemistry. Furthermore, Norman Cousins wrote a book titled *Head First: The Biology of Hope and the Healing Power of the Human Spirit*, which included studies on the effects of laughing on pain tolerance. He found that when there were laughter carts in VA hospitals for wounded soldiers, the patients required less pain medication after reading humorous books or articles that made them laugh.[2]

Perhaps the most touching proof that laughter can treat depression is what President Lincoln did while managing the Civil War. At night, he read the adventures of Artemus Ward, ingesting humor created by the writer Charles Farrar Browne so that he could have a few minutes of bed-shaking laugher. One of Lincoln's friends said that the future president told him that although he appeared to enjoy life rapturously, still he was the victim of a terrible melancholy. "He sought company and indulged in fun and hilarity without restraint…but when he was by himself…he was so overcome by mental depression that he never dared carry a knife with him."[3]

Yet when Lincoln told a funny story, his whole long, skinny frame changed. His law partner described it this way: "His power of mimicry was unique. His features seemed to take part in the performance. His gray eyes sparkled; a smile seemed to gather up, curtain-like, the corners of his mouth; his frame quivered with suppressed excitement; and when the nub of the story—as he called it—came, no one's laugh was heartier than his."[4] We Americans might could attribute his survival and the survival of our union to the laughter these stories coaxed out of Lincoln.

As for me, whenever I am asked how I learned to write stories that are funny, it's an easy answer. You see, my mother lived her life as if every day she were on the *I Love Lucy* show. Whenever she sent me to the grocery store for a loaf of bread, I was expected to come back with a funny story. It was not the bread she needed—it was the story. She fought a lifelong battle against depression, and stories were her elixir. I tend to collect these now too. Funny stories are my wrapped candies to take out and suck on when the light gets dim.

Some of my funniest stories come from audience members after I've given a talk about writing. A few years ago, a woman came up to me and gave me a doozy. She had a mother who was one hundred years old and had just gone to her doctor for a checkup. Of course, everyone was eager to ask how the visit to her doctor had gone. The next day when the daughter called her to ask, her mother said, "It was awful. Perfectly horrendous. *He* looked terrible."

Another jim-dandy came in a writing workshop I was teaching. This one could have happened anywhere, but it is so perfectly suited to Florida, I'll leave it here. You see, some of the biggest bass in the world thrive in Florida. And since most people don't know the biggest bass are big because they are females harboring hundreds of eggs, there is a sweet irony in a naïve fisherman hooking a giant bass and bragging, "Look at this monster dude"—when in reality, he's holding up a pregnant lady bass.

It was a woman from Macclenny, a town the size of a postage stamp, who gave me this fishing story. It begins with a wildfire breaking out on her farm. Helicopters came whap-whapping overhead dangling huge buckets to scoop up water from her pond to fly over to dump on the forest fire. In her pond lived a beloved bass named Fred. Fishermen from the town often taught their grandchildren how to fish by catching Fred over and over. Fred could always be enticed near the bank by dropping a trail of breadcrumbs. Kids were taught to hook the great bass in the edge of its lip so it could be thrown back in to be caught another day. But with the helicopter bucket about to scoop Fred up, a message of panic went out over the town. Grandfathers rushed to drop breadcrumbs near the bank, and since Fred obliged just as he'd been trained, they handily netted Fred and rushed the giant bass to a pond far away.

When the fire was over, Fred was returned. He thrived, stocking the pond with other generations of bass to teach other children how to fish and be kind. Since we now have learned to educate our kids with more facts about the miracles that we share with our earth, among them that big bass are all fertilized females, Fred's name has been changed to Fredericka. And if one of her offspring ends up in a frying pan to feed a family, well, that's OK too. But the lasting lesson is that sometimes it takes a village to save a bass.

Fred and Fredericka, eyeblinks, coughs, and bursts of laughter add up to a desire to survive. And since writing funny stories was not only an inherited skill from my mother, helping to keep her alive, it also became a way to become a better writer. If you can tell a story in three minutes, you're moving in the right direction. When I started reading my little stories on National Public Radio, where I decided I'd become living proof that the station was truly for the public since they'd let even me on, I found I no longer needed to be embarrassed about my Arkansas accent. Especially when I started making a little money with it. No, I didn't fall far from my father's love of a dime. Besides, I had so many animal mouths to feed.

…they all practiced laughter as a part of their well-being, often quoting the Bible for permission, such as Job 8:21, "Fill your mouth with laughter and your lips with shouts of joy."

CHAPTER FOUR

But I'd Have
Paid Five Million

Every day I rode Skip through Blueberry Hill Farm laughing at the thrill of living out my childhood dream of becoming a cowgirl. And though my mother taught me to tell a story, it was my grandmother who was the real comedienne. She didn't try to be funny. She simply was.

What you need to know here is that I was a child so adored, so enjoyed for my quirky nature, that I wallowed in never-die love and indulgence. The most indulgence came from my grandmother, who grew up in a little Tennessee cotton town. Her father had been a Methodist circuit rider specializing in funerals, going by horseback to town after town. It was said he had a booming voice and always dressed in a Mark Twain white linen suit. He also had trembling hands that added to the effect of preaching a good funeral.

He fathered a big family of eight children that included my grandmother—and they all practiced laughter as a part of their well-being, often quoting the Bible for permission, such as Job 8:21, "Fill your mouth with laughter and your lips with shouts of joy" (NIV). Or Psalm 2:4, "The one who rules in heaven laughs" (CEB). And Psalm 30:11, "You have turned my mourning into joyful dancing. You have taken away my clothes of mourning and clothed me with joy" (NLT).

My grandmother certainly knew about that last one. Her husband had died in the Spanish flu epidemic in 1918. He was only twenty-seven. She spent long visits with us to dull the loneliness of widowhood. It was her job to get me to take a nap, and she did so by reading to me until *she* fell asleep. I was born in 1944 and given the nickname the

Screaming Mimi, after a World War II bomb.

My grandmother's voice on a story tamed me, purring with the rhythm she'd learned from reading Bible verses. She was barely five feet tall. For a long time I thought she moonlighted for the circus because she could have easily fit in the car with all those clowns. She had red-tinted hair that covered her head in permed curls like tangled noodles. She was always adjusting a garter just above her knee to hold up her stockings. And I could always see a light dusting of powder above her bosom like flour on a biscuit. She said she suffered from sinking spells and liver chills, though I never saw her have one.

She was easy to scare and had several scream levels. When she let go with one, we'd all jerk in reflex. At the sound of thunder, she'd let out a whoop and crawl under a bed. During a bad storm, she was sure that balls of fire were rolling across the lawn, but she wouldn't get out from under the bed to go look, and she wouldn't let me go look either.

In fact, I think this was my first experience of loving someone by wanting to protect them, for I'd crawl under the bed with her just to keep her company.

Since she was a grown woman when electricity, telephones, and cars came into her life, she made me work the toaster and flip every light switch. When you worked anything hooked up to electricity, she was sure it could spit a fiery tongue into your face and kill you. The fact that she made me work them, disregarding the fact that the fiery tongue could kill *me*, points to how often her sense of logic abandoned her. She believed that God, Jesus, and the fire department were watching over her and often called out to summon them. Whenever she talked on the phone, she thought the telephone mouthpiece might spit a shot of electricity straight at her. Just in case this happened, and the words she said might be her last, she kept her conversations short, to the point, and intentionally sweet.

Along with these fears, she was never able to

drive a car. Every time she tried, her knees knocked together so much, she jimmied the key in the ignition and turned off the engine. She sent many a man looking for the cause of the stalled car until one finally discovered her knocking knees.

Unfortunately, I seem to have inherited that trouble with operating a vehicle, not because of my knees knocking but because I cause road rage every time I pull onto a highway. I either go too slow or weave. At times I drive like I've been drinking and fear that a cop will stop me and order me to walk the dreaded straight line. So far, I've escaped that humiliation. Still, I run over curbs and brightly say, "Whoopsie." Once when my son was about the age of fourteen, he asked me if I ever got embarrassed driving, and I realized my grandmother's inability to get along with a car had been passed down to me. And I live with it.

* * *

Back when I was still a child, at the age of five, I began suspecting that my grandmother worried that I might be the first woman in our family to go to prison. She started taking me to Sunday school every chance she got. I think she wanted me to learn about Hell and Eternal Damnation. Instead, I heard stories that were older than even my grandmother. I can't say that I knew it then like I know it now, but I sensed that stories connect us. They let us see one another. And they last. To last so long I decided stories have to have something about them that we need. They are like air or water or a good purse.

On those days when my grandmother read to me, a curiosity about words began circling my mind. Why was a *rope* a *rope* and not a *tire*? Why was a *rock* a *rock* and not a *plum*? When I asked my grandmother who had decided what each word would mean, she said, "God. God was in charge of everything."

I felt sorry for God. He'd taken a whole lot onto Himself.

However, when I began to learn to read, stories no longer came to me only in the voice of my grandmother or in the voice of someone else. I discovered words had voices of their own. Close the book, and the voice stops. Open it again, and the voice of the storyteller begins speaking in its own unique silent language. I realized the choices of those words were like the storyteller's fingerprints. Oh, happy day! Mere mortals had written books! Lots of books, and that left room for me.

I was relieved for God. He'd written one book, a really good one. Maybe He'd said all He wanted to say in that one, and it'd taken so much out of Him, He didn't feel the need to write another. In any case, from that moment, I took the vows of a storyteller and never looked back.

Of course none of this was expressed this way in my head at the age of five, but it burrowed down in my DNA like my love for the earth, dogs and cats and horses, cheesecake, and good-hearted men.

* * *

All these years later, on the day I found that Buddy had stashed so many of my things in my neighbor's garage, I knew I had witnessed my value in Buddy's life. He was not officially mine, however. Hoppy still fed him, putting food in his bowl in the garage. We all know a dog is driven by food. I also knew he would never completely give up loyalty to the hand that fed him. Buddy would always go home to Hoppy by nightfall.

I'd been raised thinking that the way to a man's heart is to turn up naked carrying a Pyrex dish of double-meat lasagna. Educated in understanding the value of food in our world, I refused to ever use it to lure a handsome male to be under my influence. As I grew into womanhood, I discovered I wanted to be desired for my character and wit, not for some body part or my beef stew.

I knew I had to confront the issue of food in

Buddy's life. I needed a business transaction to make me his official owner. Besides, the neighborhood had finally sent a letter to Hoppy about Buddy's inserting himself as a speed bump in the road and everyone's fear that he'd likely be run over.

As I was contemplating all this, I received a phone call.

"Shelley." It was Hoppy. "Since Buddy spends every day with you, what would you say if I gave him to you?"

"Are you sure? I mean, he still looks to you as his official home."

"Yeah. But he has this thing for you. He seems to think about you all the time. When he's here, he's always looking across the street for you. And if I lock him in, he'll find a way to get out and head to find you. With Stella, it's a dog thing for him. But with you, it's something else altogether. I can't name it. Can you?"

"Well, to be honest, I'm looking into it. I've

researched dog attachment. I've found nothing, really. It's just believed that dogs often have a preference for someone, and it doesn't always have a clear reason."

"Will you take him then? Besides, I have a bit of a new complication."

There was a long moment of silence, then he blurted: "You see, I got married again, and my new wife has a Labrador retriever that Buddy beat up as soon as he saw him. If anything happens to my new wife's dog, this marriage is in trouble."

Memories of Hoppy's sorrow dripping off him after his first wife left him still haunted me. I quickly said, "I'd love to have Buddy. Do you think we should make up a bill of sale, something legal?" I was actually worrying about my own heart as much as Buddy's heart. I can't give away anything that I've fallen in love with. I knew he couldn't give me up either.

Hoppy answered, "I don't think a bill of sale is necessary. I'll never challenge your ownership no matter what happens. Besides, how much could we claim he is worth?" He laughed. His laugh was a good laugh. His will to live was percolating.

I bit my tongue to keep from saying *five million dollars*; not that I had it, but it was a sort-of measure of what Buddy meant to me. I replied instead, "Done."

"Done," he echoed.

Hoppy walked over with Buddy on a leash. I was behind the barn giving Skip a bath.

Hoppy came close, unleashed Buddy, and said, "He's all yours." Hoppy then headed home.

Right away, Buddy turned around and followed Hoppy back across the road. The snap releasing the leash from his collar was not the signal Buddy needed. He knew where his food bowl was.

I was not insulted. Buddy would come back after he'd been fed to spend the night on my front porch, waiting for me to appear in the morning. I would have to come up with a way to brand Buddy as mine.

We each accepted who we were, and that was that. We could never let those differences come between us.

CHAPTER FIVE

Lipstick

My search was on. Why did Buddy choose me over all the other *Homo sapiens* on the street? My first research led me to Darwin. Over one hundred fifty years ago as our renowned natural scientist, Darwin published his theory that all animals, including humans, show emotion in similar ways. For instance, both humans and animals purse lips during concentration. We can both show anger by narrowing our eyes—which today we like to describe as giving someone the stink eye. And, like animals, we can show our teeth in anger. In addition, while listening intently, both animals and humans often let their mouths hang open.

When Darwin was writing up his theories, no one liked what he was saying because no one liked being compared to an animal. But for Darwin, considering these shared behaviors between animals and humans was living proof that we had a common ancestry, which he wrote about in his famous book *The Descent of Man*.

During the 1970s, psychologist Paul Eckman got into the act, expanding Darwin's work on emotions, identifying six basic emotions in all human cultures: happiness, sadness, disgust, fear, surprise, and anger. Right away I tried to see them all in Buddy so I could joke that he was as human as I was. I'd seen him radiate happiness at the sight of me, though he wasn't a gusher. He was more like ET in that movie about an extraterrestrial whose heart glowed red to show love.

Similarly, you could feel Buddy's heart beating with bliss whenever I came near. In essence, he was a stoic—a John Wayne-type of dog, or a Rocky Balboa. If he thought someone was giving me the stink eye, he'd look at that person with his yellow eyes rimmed in pink threatening to gnaw their arm like a T-bone. His size, which was about 125 pounds, promised stitches to whoever put me at risk. For the decade we were together, I often fancied taking him to walk beside me through the bad part of New York's Central Park or the Tenderloin district of San Francisco, to gloat at drug dealers' and rapists' bug-eyed stares as they decided Buddy was not worth tangling with. I wouldn't need to use a leash either. Unless I was taking him to the vet, he always hugged my side like a suckerfish. It was always astonishing to me, too, that whenever we arrived at the vet's office, the first thing the vet people do—you know—is put your dog on a scale. Well, I couldn't lift Buddy, so I simply pointed to the scale and said, "Get on that thing, Buddy," then watched as he did, while everyone in the office gawked and laughed in stupefied wonder.

Since his tail wasn't the substitute for a hug or smile, it was more like a part of his uniform, like the badge on a lovesick bodyguard. The fact that

I inhabited the same planet with him was all he needed to be calm, thankful, and steadfast. But if I were gone, like to the grocery store, I was told that he'd crawl up into the big wicker chair on the porch with his tail drooping and his eyes glazed over until he saw my car coming. He would always meet me as I pulled into the garage.

His ears were the fold-over kind, like the flap on an envelope, so when he was ashamed after turning over the garbage can, his ears would pinch against his head in apology. I'd seen him display disgust after going for a Burger King Whopper he found in a ditch and then smelled that it was rotten. (As for the other human emotions of fear, surprise, and anger, we'll get to those in a minute.)

On that first day when Hoppy brought him over on a leash to be mine and then Buddy followed Hoppy home, my most pressing thought was how to make Buddy know he was mine. I needed to signal that he would no longer need to go to Hoppy's to be fed. Of course, just feeding him would make that point. Expressing love is a whole other matter.

Similar to the way I admit that I write my awful rhymes on purpose to be funny, I declare myself to be a damn good kisser. But then, to really know, you'd have to interview those I kiss. So far, I have not done that. I'm afraid to hear the truth. Nonetheless, I take pride in my kissing ability and often wear lipstick to brand those I love. I even buy lipstick shades at the grocery store like I would collect art supplies. One of the most fun things in life is to think up lipstick colors, such as Firecracker Red, Scarlet Harlot, Commie Red, Full-Bank-Account Wine, Drunk Cardinal, Beet Juice Insane…I chose Crazy-in-Love Ruby for Buddy.

On that first day of our official ownership of each other, as soon as Buddy came back from Hoppy's after having his supper, I planted a kiss on his forehead and said aloud, "Now you are Buddy Mickle, and don't you ever doubt it."

When I invited him inside the house, he wore the brand of my lips as he picked out a spot beside my bed to sleep. It was a place where his back would be against a wall. He was like one of those gunfighters in an old Western movie, always sitting with his back to a wall so he couldn't be snuck up on.

In his presence, my life swelled and changed. I fed on daily fat slices of happiness. And every day, as the object of my joy, Buddy wore the shape of my lips on his forehead as my brand.

He and I fought about only one thing: He liked the way he smelled, and I didn't. When he sensed I was going to give him a bath, he ran and hid. He'd scoot under my car or the truck or run into the boxwood hedge near the barn. He knew I'd bend down to look under the truck and when my eyes met his yellow snake eyes, he'd give up and let me poke him out with a rake handle. If he took off to the boxwoods, he always forgot that his hog-sized end zone would not fit. It was really pitiful to see him thinking he was totally hidden when nothing of the sort could have been further from the truth. I'd lasso him with Skip's lead rope to drag him out. I showered him behind the barn to protect his modesty and put Old Spice in his rinse water.

Now that I was counting Buddy's display of the six emotions that psychologist Paul Eckman said are universally shared among humans, I saw him exhibit real surprise on the day I came up on him when I was running the vacuum cleaner. As usual, I was handling the machine in a devil-may-care style while Buddy was asleep on the screen porch. He was so startled, he sprang through the screen paneling, leaving a Buddy-sized hole.

I saw him display anger only when a stray dog came into the yard. He clamped his bulldog jaws around the visiting dog's snout and bit down. However, the day he showed me his other human trait of surprise was one of the worst days of my life.

* * *

It was spring; the woods animals were giving birth.

A baby rabbit came hopping out of a thicket heading across the yard. Before I realized what could happen, Buddy jumped into a full run and snapped the little fellow up. When I yelled no at him, he looked at me with a sort of sorry-but-not-really-sorry look. He was a carnivore, born to hunt. Now I was faced with the most profound dilemma a human faces: what to do about the suffering?

The baby bunny was paralyzed, its back legs dangling when I picked it up. I was alone at the farm. I would have to make a terrible decision.

I had to put the little fellow out of its misery. It could not have any sort of life that would allow it to thrive, and I could not tolerate its suffering. Yet I couldn't bear to do the deed by bludgeoning it to death. I had to think of a way to end its suffering that would not require a violent act on my part. My brain churned, even asking myself if this were me, how would I prefer to die? I finally took Skip's water bucket, filled it at the faucet behind the barn, and submerged the little rabbit in it. When all life was clearly gone, I took a spade and dug the best hole I could in the Florida clay. I kissed the little rabbit and put it in. I covered it with dirt.

After I finished my dreaded deed, I went in the house for a beer to calm my nerves. Within an hour, Buddy dug into the shallow grave and ran off with the prey that had unlocked his carnivorous instincts, which then had led to the rabbit murder. His energy and ability to thrive came from eating the tissues of other animals. Whereas I, as an omnivore, was able to digest both plants and meat, putting me somewhere between Buddy and Skip, who lived on the lush pastures of Blueberry Hill Farm and store-bought grain. This was the moment when Buddy and I had to recognize our differences and live them out without ever trying to change each other or deny our natures.

We each accepted who we were, and that was that. We could never let those differences come between us.

I fell in love with an Arkansas cotton town that consisted of one paved main street and a half dozen gravel side roads, surrounded by miles of flat dusty land that grew cotton and rice and soybeans about as well as Michael Jordan could dunk a basketball, which says a lot about a human's need to love wherever we find ourselves.

CHAPTER SIX

Lightn'

Long ago I learned that projecting human feelings onto an animal is a dead end. Anthropomorphism is best left as a word in a dictionary, even though I had sought to witness Buddy displaying the human emotions people share. Besides, half the time we are wrong when we ascribe human feelings to an animal, which an Arkansas plowhorse taught me.

You see, back when ten cents could get you into the movies, your family could get rid of you for a few hours while you sat in a double feature of a cowboy movie. My first crush was on Roy Rogers and equally on Trigger. Apparently, there's a good bit written down by Freud and people like that about girls and horses, and that the connection between them is based on something sexual. In my opinion all that is a bunch of hooey because I know something about growing up female. I know that what girls most want to learn from horses has to do with survival.

Any horse manual you pick up will tell you that if you're leading one and the darn thing balks, make him step in a different direction—even reach out and push his shoulder if you have to, just get him off balance—then lead him to where you really want him to go. The point is not to ever let him know his own strength. Managing a thousand-pound animal takes finesse. If he refuses to do something you have asked him to do, tuck one of his ears under the top strap of his bridle or halter, and by the time he gets it loose, he'll have forgotten what he didn't want to do in the first place. Remember, body posture is everything. Act like you know what you're doing and where you are going, and he'll be inclined to follow you.

I can truthfully say that all of these techniques I have used on a horse at one time or another, and also at one time or another on some person, most often a man. And certainly as a mother with a toddler, I used it all the time.

I have never lost my passion for horses. It was so bad while I was growing up, my family got tired of me talking about horses all the time. They sometimes told me, not even politely, to "shut up." It got so bad that finally when I was twelve, they said I could cash in some of my college U.S. savings bonds to buy a horse. And my best friend's dad said he'd keep a horse for me free so his daughter would have someone to ride with.

We were a family without means. Land rich but cash poor. Anything that smacked of luxury was off the table. With my parents coming out of the Great Depression, when asking for charity would be the worst shame for a middle-class family, we lived close to the bone.

To have all this make sense, you have to see where we were living. We'd moved by then to the tiny cotton town in Arkansas where my father grew up so he could help care for his parents. He opened a construction company to build back whatever tornadoes knocked down. I put an ad in our local paper: *Girl, 12, wants a horse. All possibilities considered.*

One day a knock came on the back door. A farmer with tobacco-stained teeth and wearing overalls said he had a retired plowhorse he'd let me have for seventy-five dollars. "What's her name?" I asked.

"Lightn'," he replied. "She's fast."

My parents drove me out to the cotton farm where he lived to meet Lightn'. When I got out of the car, the farmer changed the price for the mare to eighty-five dollars, which was my first lesson in horse-trading. I sized her up: bay with a white heart shape on her forehead; a bottom lip hanging down so far below her top one that a congregation of flies was hanging out in there; and, most impressive, a white streak in her black mane where the plow harness had killed the hair roots. The signs of having lived a hard, fun-free life were everywhere on her. Her eyes were dazed; her head hung low. Clearly she had given up on life long ago and was as sour as an old kumquat. But for a twelve-year-old girl, she was perfect. No one thought she had enough energy to kill me. Besides, from the first moment that I saw her, my heart swelled and purred. I loved her fiercely.

I'd had enough riding lessons in various places to think I could try her out there and then. I was happily naïve about what a horse can do to you. The farmer picked me up and set me down in his saddle that I swear dated from the Civil War. It was then that he told me she'd started out in her life with him bearing the name Nell, which was also the name of his wife. I rode Lightn'Nell around the barn with her hooves sinking in mud. When I squeezed my legs against her, she instantly trotted, a good sign that she was not as worn out as she looked, or at least wanted to get the hell out of where she was.

I bought her and soon found out for myself where she got her second name. After spending more than a decade plowing cotton fields, she was so quick to get out of one that if I rode her in a race with my friends using the rows of cotton to keep us from running into each other, my eighty-five-dollar horse would win every time. Not even the flies could keep up.

Since this little town stole my heart and wrapped it in a memory cloth to stay warm in my mind through all these years, it is important that you feel it. For most likely you feel the same way about somewhere, tucked away in your past. That I fell in love with an Arkansas cotton town that consisted of one paved main street and a half dozen gravel side roads, surrounded by miles of flat, dusty land that grew cotton and rice and soybeans about as well as Michael Jordan could dunk a basketball, says a lot about a human's need to love wherever we find ourselves. I licked the vision of the earth as steadily as a pasture animal standing over a block of salt, while at the same time soaking in its sounds to instinctively make of nature my serenity—a source of renewal and strength.

On the side of the highway when you drove in was a sign: McCrory, Arkansas, pop. 1,115. When someone was born, I assumed someone died, because the number on the sign never changed. The fact that I was impervious to the hardscrabble lives being lived around me, to the low buzz of the Jim Crow culture that kept me barricaded from deeply knowing and spending time with people I loved, was not yet a troublesome throb in my awareness. I was still learning; my eyesight was locked into the range of a child, not yet attuned to what was in my peripheral vision. I saw only what was in front of me—mostly the miracles of nature, including what the mare, Lightn'Nell, was teaching me.

She tried to bite me every time I got on. When I walked into the pasture to catch her, she'd rush to stand next to the bull. When we rode through woods, she'd pick out the lowest limb to run under to scrape me off.

The bald truth is, nothing she did could ever dint my love for her. I'm not going to say that her hateful traits made me love her less, or in a crazy way, to love her even more. But I am going to say that nothing she ever did made me want to get rid of her. My friends made fun of me because I wrote her love letters and asked them to read them to her when I was out of town. Even now I'm not afraid of you knowing all this because I consider being crazy in love—with a human, an animal, with the earth, or a dream—something to be proud of.

And how wrong I would have been to practice anthropomorphism in trying to understand my worn-out mare. For, now, after being alive for a good long while, I know what most likely she was thinking when she saw me coming toward her with a bridle to catch her and ride her half to death: *Here comes the little bitch.* When she half reared just enough to get me to slide off into a muddy ditch, she was thinking, *Sorry, kid, but you're on my last nerve.* And when she wrapped her mouth around my skinny thigh while I was getting on, yet never clamped down, she was clearly deciding, *This kid really needs to take a bath, but I'm gonna let her live another day.*

No, anthropomorphism is a dangerous business. It's sometimes best to not know what your dog, cat, pig, goat, or horse is thinking about you.

* * *

Now, here, I'm going to introduce you to Verna Mae because if anyone deserves to be in a book, she does. You see, when I was teaching myself how to write, I read every good writer's work that I could get my hands on. And one of those writers said that he thought of death as being like a page in a book that no one was reading. So if I have not pissed you off too bad so far, you're still reading and now you'll get to know the miracle of Verna Mae.

No one could love more completely than she loved. And that love fed her magnanimous ability to forgive. She had been working for my family for years. She came to our house through the back door as was the custom for those who wore the title of maid. Coming to the front door was a no-no for anyone with her skin color. And she came several times a week to cook, clean, do laundry, and exercise my storytelling muscle.

She shelled peas and fried pork chops. She pushed around a hot iron on my laundered cotton dresses while sprinkling the ruffles with water out of a soda-pop bottle. While she worked, we'd spin a tale together, adding, as needed, sound effects for our ghost stories. Verna Mae had the best bloodcurdling screams and the sound of chains being dragged that I've ever come across. She could flop her tongue in the sound of a horse galloping in a quick getaway, and our imaginations synced in perfect rhythm. We always performed our storytelling when no one else was in the house—not that we were ashamed of our sound effects or tale spinning; it was just that we knew we'd become a joke. Our understanding could not be risked.

The winter after I bought Nell, the wonderful, kind man who had volunteered to keep her for me turned her out for the winter in the big pasture where he kept his cattle herd. The Arkansas winters could be cruel to a kid thirsting to ride her horse on the miles of dirt roads that surrounded the town. I pestered my mother enough about wanting to go catch Nell that she finally told me, "Oh, all right then. Go get in the station wagon." It was one of those paneled station wagons with real wood that was turning to the shade of a ripening banana. We were actually starting to worry about termites. My mother told Verna Mae to get in too.

Out in the big pasture, we chased after Nell. I was carrying a halter to slip over her head once we got her cornered. But Nell was smarter than any of us. She trotted circles around us, getting closer each time, then bolted off to stand by the bull, who had a mean look and a scary reputation. After about an hour of this horse–human tag, my mother lost patience as Nell trotted by and yelled, "Verna Mae, get her!" Verna Mae did a flying tackle and grabbed Nell by the ears. She wrestled the old sour mare into a pretzel shape while hanging on until I got there with the halter. As usual, once caught, Nell became a pussycat, following me back to the barn for the saddle as if saying, *Wadn't that fun?*

Not many days later, my mother needed an ingredient for something she was cooking and sent me to Verna Mae's house to ask to borrow it. That cup-of-sugar thing, you know. It was the first time

I'd seen where Verna Mae lived, the first glimpse of *her* life. She knew mine completely, but her life was a mystery, one that I had not even been curious about until that day. In town was one street where all the Black people lived. And there in the unpainted wood house where Verna Mae lived with her daughter who was about my age but did not go to my school—I got what I was sent for. The differences in the way we lived struck me with a harshness that didn't make sense. Verna Mae didn't have a phone. She didn't have a car. Probably no one paid money into her Social Security to prevent the poverty of old age. So when she got old, she'd be on her own. She was depending on the kindness of her employers, the families whose dishes she washed, whose children she helped raise, to answer her most urgent needs. Not a good way to live. It was the direct opposite of what I was being taught by my father's fear of being without financial security. I saw the difference in our lives and the way it was overlooked as if this difference was simply the way things should be.

In time, I realized that Verna Mae had the most unusual ability to finish your sentences with you as you said the last words. For instance, if you said, "I went to the five-and-dime today because I needed a new pencil," she'd pick up that sentence with you so that together you'd say "needed a new…" and then she'd echo "pencil" after you said "pencil." In essence she was joining up with you in the sweet form of a sentence duet. It took smarts. It was her form of survival in the Jim Crow culture that separated us in all public places. It also conveyed her affection. She was giving us a hardy dose of forgiveness for the way our culture squashed her life and confined it by laws and customs that dictated her everyday existence.

For instance, we had a movie theater downtown that we loved, where a whole posse of us kids would crowd in every Saturday. A door beside the main entrance opened from the sidewalk onto a staircase, where if you did not have white skin, you entered, passed the candy counter with its back side ready to serve those going up to the balcony. White children bought candy from the other side. In that theater, if Verna Mae were ever to accompany me to a movie, she would have to sit up there—separated from me and the other white children downstairs as we cheered on the movie-screen stars who galloped after bad guys to put them in the slammer.

Not long after I figured out the difference between my life and Verna Mae's, I found a carpenter's level in a vacant lot. "Look what I found." I showed it to Verna Mae while she was in the kitchen ironing. I held out the carpenter's level and sat down on a stool by the counter. Verna Mae put down the iron and held the level to take a good look. "Interesting looking thing, isn't it?"

Indeed it was. It was a wooden plank with a little bubble in a tube that could slide between three different marked sections. Get the bubble in the middle, and whatever you are setting the plank on is said to be level. If the bubble slides to either the right section or the left, then it is off-kilter, and you better not nail down what you were about to nail down.

"What you going to do with it?" Verna Mae asked.

"I'm not sure yet, but I know I'm going to keep it."

I took it to my father and asked him to saw it down to the size of a small box. He did, and I took it to my room where in privacy I used a red pen to write *nuts* over the left side of the section of the tube, and then *sane* over the middle part, and *haywire* over the right section. I looked up the words in the dictionary to make sure I spelled them right. Then I went back to my father sitting at his desk. "Can I try this out on you?" I asked.

"Sure," he said but kept working his adding machine.

I set the carpenter rule on his head. His thick hair held it steady. The bubble moved right away into the middle part, *sane*. He reached up and touched my crazy meter. "What you got there?"

I took it off his head and let him hold it. He chuckled. "So how did I turn out?"

"Right in the middle," I reported. "Levelheaded. Sane as sane can be."

"Well, try it again." He held his head very still. I set the crazy meter once again on top. He tilted his head to the left, and the bubble in the plank slid off into *nuts* quicker than a sneeze.

"*Nuts* it says this time," I told him.

"I thought so," he chuckled again. "Go try it on your mother."

My mother was cleaning out a closet. Her lipstick was as bright as the wings of a male cardinal. "I've come to measure you," I said.

"Measure what?"

"The inside of your head."

She didn't step out of the closet, instead bent over and said, "Go to it."

"I think you better sit down," I warned her.

"I'm too busy. Just do whatever you're doing, here and now."

"You're going to regret it," I advised her.

"I am?"

She figured I was up to something that was going to be worth a laugh and a story in the long run.

She sat down, and I set the crazy meter on top of her head, and it slipped over into *haywire* so fast, it was ridiculous. "I was afraid so," I said.

"Afraid of what?" She now reached up to her head, held my crazy meter, and laughed out loud. "Lord-a-mercy! This is the funniest thing I've seen all week. Who else have you tried it on?"

"Daddy."

"And?" Her eyes grew big. Her eyebrows shot up.

"Sane at first. Then nuts."

"S'what I've always figured." She handed me back my crazy meter. "Go try it on your grandparents."

Over the next week, I kept a running tally from all over town. It was strange how anybody who measured *sane* first, quickly tipped their heads to get over into *nuts* or *haywire*. The bubble in the crazy meter plank slid back and forth between all sections. It was quite clear: everybody living in my own time and place was ashamed of coming up sane.

Even more important, the concept of shapeshifting means that each of us can shift into being more of the self we want to be. In essence, a better version of ourselves.

Shapeshifting

Living on Blueberry Hill Farm, I craved company and good conversation. Even though I am not a good cook, I began throwing dinner parties. *Throwing* is exactly the right verb, for it more or less added up to slinging hash as I tossed ingredients together and hoped they wouldn't poison anybody. Thinking I had become OK on a few recipes, I invited professors from the university and others I met who piqued my interest, always on the search for a quirky conversation. When not many turned down my invitations, I became confident that I could put on a dinner party without having my guests swallow a handful of Tums on the way home.

Buddy sat at my feet under the table. Since

he was so big that his head hit the underside of the dining table, he naturally caught the respect of my guests. And everyone noticed his allegiance to me. Several even commented that his bond to me was extraordinary. They noticed that he would do whatever I told him to, like move out from under the table or get off the couch when he tried to sit beside a guest during appetizer hour.

Lest you think he was perfect, I'll declare that once when I went to greet an arriving guest, Buddy ate all the appetizers on the coffee table while my back was turned. But he didn't do it again. I let him know that had been a no-no. I had taught him the basics such as "Sit," "Stay," and "Lie down." But generally he didn't need my words. He intuitively read my mind. Our language was as silent as the act of my writing in what I called "having words in my fingers." I often wondered how I could write words I couldn't even pronounce—a mystery that intrigues me even now. Go figure.

At one dinner party, a physicist commented, "I think that dog is a polyglot." Since I didn't know what that was, I nodded and said, "No doubt." But then my guest began speaking Japanese, and Buddy seemed to understand him, too, looking at him with rapt attention. It then became a running joke for others to speak to Buddy in whatever foreign language they knew. We all laughed together as the same idea popped into our heads: Buddy was a polyglot passing as a dog.

"What if he is shapeshifting?" one guest suggested.

Like the word *polyglot* I had to look that up later too. In the most elemental terms, I found shapeshifting to be defined as a way to extend one's own human senses to experience the world through another shape. I found a book titled *Shapeshifting* by John Perkins. And since what he says is so interesting, I won't paraphrase but quote verbatim: "Throughout history we humans have found shapeshifting to be one of the most effective means for transforming ourselves. A Lakota Sioux warrior shapeshifted into a buffalo in order to become a better hunter and to honor the spirit of an animal that provided his family with food, clothing, bowstrings, and fuel."[5] In more elemental terms it means imagining walking around in some other skin. Even more important, the concept of shapeshifting means that each of us can shift into being more of the self we want to be. In essence, a better version of ourselves.

Furthermore, Perkins points out that when Neil Armstrong stepped on the moon and uttered the words, "One small step for man, one giant leap for mankind," the sentence conveyed that the real leap was deep inside our psyches.[6] We entered a realm that offers an extraordinary opportunity for us to change ourselves. Most importantly for me, Perkins emphasizes that storytelling is part of the shapeshifter's tradition, allowing us to imagine being someone else.

I took the understanding that Buddy had shapeshifted himself into me as he tried to do everything to please me, and, as I anticipated his needs and desires, I shapeshifted into him.

Whatever else Buddy and I had together in forms of communications and shared love would have to be chalked up to a mystery, a mystery as much as the concept of shapeshifting that had been practiced for centuries between living things and nonliving things, expressing hopes. But it worked. Buddy and I were transforming each other. I was receiving his love without questioning it. I was becoming kinder, and he was...well, I venture to say he was deliciously happy for the first time in his life for the simplest of reasons: he was expressing love and having that love received and returned. Loving me was giving him the job he craved.

Yet I still wanted to understand more about what we had together. Is that really any different from any relationship when an unexpected love comes along?

I recently had a second profound experience of shapeshifting that came from my having lived so long. You see, I think Neil Armstrong's famous quote has been revised. When he said that stepping on the moon was a huge step for mankind, today he'd know better and say, "A huge step for *humankind*," so as not to leave anyone out. I might have even edited his statement to say: a huge step for women, dogs, cats, horses, and all other animal earthlings.

*Every woman should
know how to pump
her own gas.*

CHAPTER EIGHT

Pumping Gas

I learned a lot about myself as a woman that first summer on Blueberry Hill Farm. Every woman should know how to pump her own gas. And I practiced my belief religiously. I drove to the nearby gas station to fill up my used Lincoln Town Car. "Used" is a word I do not like. I prefer "previously loved." "Used books" should be recategorized as "previously loved" books. "Used cars" should be "previously loved" cars. And my Lincoln Town Car had certainly been loved.

When I'd had to give up the station wagon that had hauled kids here and there, I had to buy a car with a trunk big enough to hold my western saddle. Few cars have a trunk that big. That saddle weighed thirty-eight pounds of carved leather trimmed in silver. Since becoming a cowgirl, I've always shopped for a car from the trunk up. I have salesmen open the trunk rather than the hood. And if my saddle won't fit, I move on.

That's why I chose one of those Lincoln Town Cars, which feels most like riding in a boat. It was white with blue velvet upholstery. I named it Madonna. Lest you think I'm crazier than I admit, I name all my appliances. The fridge is Rufus; the dishwasher Henry; the washing machine Earle. Rufus is a problem at night because when he makes ice to drop in the bin, he moans.

That morning I needed gas in Madonna. I invited Buddy to ride along. I opened the back door, and instantly he got in, then quickly jumped into the front seat to ride shotgun. As usual, he was wearing the shape of my lips in the shade of Crazy-in-Love Ruby on his pickle-jar-sized head.

Now, get ready, because I'm going to confess my most detestable trait. I can blame it on my grandmother whose hobby was people-watching, categorizing everyone she saw as either high class, common, or outright trashified. So in that vein, I generally assume that everyone is an asshole until proven otherwise—the proof being to display at least 75 percent of a warm heart and pending admission into, and full belief in, the Beloved Community.

Over the years I've collected knowledge about what a warm heart is. When I witness someone perform an act of kindness or generosity, I qualify them as having a warm heart. But the most fun description comes from the first year I moved to Florida, when I knew that Marjorie Kinnan Rawlings was its most revered writer and read everything she had written, which included the description of one of her characters who said about someone, *She has a heart as big as her behind.* And another who visited a desperately poor pregnant woman and later reported, *She ain't got nobody looking out for her but me and the Lord, and He ain't exactly put hisself out lately.* That was enough for me, and I now use those measurements most often in measuring the size of someone's heart.

On the day I was going to put gas in Madonna, as I was about to put my despicable practices on display, I parked by the gas pump and was shooting gas into Madonna's tank when two men drove up in a dually—one of those trucks that has two rear wheels on each side. They got out and began walking toward me. I was assuming that like some others whom I'd quickly categorized as assholes, they were about to suggest that I put one of those leather collars with spikes on Buddy. He looked like that kind of dog. He was always a victim of profiling. I knew it, but also knew he would be insulted to be seen that way. The size of his patoot qualified him in Marjorie Kinnan Rawlings's measurement as having a big heart.

Instead, the two men looked in at Buddy and didn't touch the glass window. They respectfully held back from teasing him to lunge or bark and said simply, "Nice dog, lady." Then they closely looked at me, taking in the whole of me, not in a critical way but with a twinkle in their eye. I had spurs on my riding boots because I'd just ridden Skip and he always needed encouragement. His lazy disposition made him loath to go anywhere. His idea of a good time was to stand under a shade tree and rest one back foot. Then another. His laziness also made him safe. To buck me off or whirl and bolt would take too much effort. So I was always safe riding him. Now one of my perceived assholes was looking intently at my spurs. He grinned and said, "You're my kind of woman."

All three of us instantly burst out laughing. Yeah, I know, I could have been insulted and taken it as an inappropriate comment, but it was just so lusciously funny. We simply loved sharing the moment for what it was.

Not long after, telling the tale to others to

make them laugh, I realized that I was as much an asshole as I'd assumed those men were. As far as its definition goes, the dictionary says an asshole is someone who is narrow-minded, who will quickly stomp on your dreams as soon as you express them, who will pretend to like you when they don't—in other words, a classic phony in the sense of Holden Caulfield's definition of a phony in *Catcher in the Rye*. There is also—believe it or not—a term called assholism. At one time or another we all suffer from it, and I was no exception. I had sized them up with my own prejudices. Assholism can be contagious.

After I pumped my gas, I drove home, put another lipstick declaration of love on Buddy's forehead, and galloped Skip across a sunset pasture. That inheritance thing—that what we see is what we were taught—was worrisome. Not only had my beloved grandmother been an avid people-watcher, she also practiced intolerance, mostly based on her interpretation of the Bible. She believed literally in that passage in Genesis 9, verses 18 to 27 that begins with what we know about Noah. When he came off the ark, he had three sons: Shem, Ham, and Japheth. Since everyone else was dead from the flood, these three would repopulate the whole earth. One day, Noah got drunk and fell asleep naked. Ham saw him and told his brothers. If he was giggling, neither my grandmother nor the Bible said. But anyway, the story goes that Shem and Japheth politely took a blanket, laid it on both their shoulders, and walked backward to cover their naked father with it. All the time, they were turning their faces away so they wouldn't see Noah in his embarrassing position.

When Noah woke up and realized what his youngest son, Ham, had done, he was furious. He put a curse on Ham's son, Canaan, saying all the children of Canaan and his children's children would be slaves forever, which is what my grandmother and many other Southerners quoted to rationalize the Jim Crow laws that separated the races.

My other grandmother was a Mississippi blueblood who had two brothers who fought in the Civil War. She told me they'd been bivouacked in Canton, which I didn't question because it sounded so much like they'd had something sexual done to them. But my point is, my Mississippi grandmother believed the same as my other grandmother: that Black people didn't mind being slaves; they were so happy! Why, just listen to them sing! I began to see that my grandmothers completely overlooked the fact that since Noah's sons repopulated the earth after the flood, we were all related to one another, which included even Verna Mae. I didn't point that out, since I didn't want to be responsible for giving my grandmothers sinking spells and liver chills, but it sure demonstrated the fact that you could lift words off a page and interpret them to mean anything.

My grandmothers also told me that anybody who was not Protestant and white loved sex more than anything. So Protestants had to work doubly hard to keep Catholics, Jews, and Black people from outnumbering us.

I loved my grandmothers. But I could not in any way join up with their view of the world.

This was my first lesson in knowing that we can love someone while also detesting their beliefs. Like Buddy, who had been longing to have a home, I had passed the first hard test of being a human in a family that would always think differently than me. Buddy and I both could love in a way that might be called "in spite of."

I realized Buddy was the witness of my life, my collaborator. . . He would be the one who could most accurately tell the story of my life. . .

CHAPTER NINE

Saving Each Other

The spring when we'd been living on Blueberry Hill Farm for more than a year, the family of a little boy called to ask if he could come see Dr. Mickle as part of his eighth birthday celebration. That little boy had been one of my husband's patients. He had suffered from an astrocytoma, a tumor in the cerebellum, the part of the brain that controls, among other things, balance and coordination. Luckily his tumor had been benign.

He and his family came driving up in the afternoon, and after a hearty visit in which their memories of the illness, surgery, and recovery were shared, the little boy saw Skip in the pasture and asked if he could ride. "Of course," I said, and went out and caught Skip to saddle him and bring him up to the round pen behind the barn. (A round pen is like a small corral, a circle of fencing with a diameter of fifty feet or so that is used for training.)

The little boy had a scar like a zipper on the back of his neck. I put my big western saddle on Skip, and my husband picked the little boy up and set him in it. Buddy sat down outside the round pen to watch. The little boy's balance was obviously unsteady so he held on to the saddle horn while wearing a wide grin. Skip was as caring and gentle as a horse ever is, slowly following the path near the fence where I had practiced horse whispering, talking to him in his own language. Skip didn't need that extra training, but I did. I needed to feel proficient as a cowgirl. Skip knew about a half dozen words and sounds, such as *walk*, *trot*, *whoa*, *canter*, and *back*. He also read my body language as well as Buddy did. When I gave the command *walk,* Skip sauntered carefully around the round pen while I stood in the center. When the little guy had been around a few times, I said, "When you're ready to stop, tell him to W-H-O-A." I spelled it so he'd be the one to give the command that Skip knew only too well. The little boy said in an apologetic sweet voice, "I don't know what that spells."

I myself often had trouble with it. After all, it's a damn hard word to spell. But by the time the little guy finished his admission, Skip had stopped. Skip could spell better than all of us.

We laughed. Skip stood stone still, feeling the little boy's precarious balance, and looked toward me, satisfied. Buddy still sat quietly at the gate of the round pen, ready to usher us back to the barn. The little boy was lifted down, and I turned Skip back out to graze the rest of the afternoon.

As I looked Buddy in the eye, answering the question that the little boy had asked as to why that big dog had red on his forehead, I realized Buddy was the witness of my life, my collaborator. We would finish out our relationship over the rest of that decade. He would be the one who could most accurately tell the story of my life in that time.

Before the little boy went home, he uttered to my husband, "Thank you for making me OK."

At only eight, he already knew that profound realization. But he was only half right. We were saving each other—my husband by feeling his value in having the surgical know-how to save a life, and me, by banking the joy in seeing the little boy's bliss that would become a future story. From that boy's serenity, which he put on display that day, I recalled another great truth that I had gleaned through Marjorie Kinnan Rawlings's classic novel *The Yearling*. When the main character, Jody Baxter, suffers the great blow of his pet deer's death, Jody's father says, "Life goes back on us. You have to take it for your share and go on."[7]

Clearly that day, displaying the universal truth of that novel, my husband's patient had taken his unlucky blow of a brain tumor as being his share and shelved it in his mind as something that had once happened but was not to be chewed over for any future length of time.

Joseph Campbell, that great guru who guided the screenwriters of the Star Wars movies, and who also wrote *The Power of Myth,* told us that stories don't tell us the meaning of life—they tell us how to live in the world.

That little guy already knew that.

Until my own Overview Effect kicked in, I never would have searched out the intricacies of America's founding to try to understand who we are, to realize that we are all traveling in the same direction, that we are all hanging on to spaceship Earth—and that I should love those crowding my space, even those with whom I heartily disagree.

CHAPTER TEN

Looking in Outer Space

Still wanting to understand how Buddy and I had leapt across the divide of our species, I found the work of space philosopher Frank White. For years, he collected stories of astronauts telling their experiences in space because he believes that storytelling is a tool for social transformation. He found some astronauts who had experienced a cognitive shift, a new awareness. That is, they went up into space as one person and came back as someone else. It's what we often call being changed from the inside out. That experience became known as the Overview Effect. It was soon considered "a message to humanity about who we are, where we are in the universe, and where we are going."[8]

While the experiences of different astronauts were expressed differently, their collective stories added up to new information. In a nutshell, the Overview Effect becomes the hard realization that we're all in this together.

Scott Carpenter called his Mercury mission "the supreme experience of my life."[9] The feeling of being released from gravity became a new concept of freedom. Carpenter found the sight of the earth from space overwhelming. He saw cloud formations that any painter could be proud of—rosettes or clustered circles of fair-weather cumulous blue. He could look off for perhaps a thousand miles in any direction. Everywhere he looked, through the window and periscope, was filled with beauty. "I took pictures as fast as I could, and as I raced towards night…I saw the beginnings of the most fantastically beautiful view I have ever had—my first sunset in space. Everything was so new and so awe-inspiring that it was difficult to concentrate for very long on any one thing."[10]

Walter Schirra gave remarkable detail from an orbit at a distance of 101 miles. He said he could see houses in the Himalayan mountains, Tibet, and the southwestern areas of the United States. He claimed to see smoke rising from the chimneys of individual houses in Tibet and the lakes near Johnson Space Center in Houston.[11] He admitted: "Of all the preparations I had made, there is no way you can be prepared for the emotional impact."[12] Shuttle astronaut Don Lind said that there was no way to prepare for the Overview Effect.[13]

Furthermore, those who experienced these emotional changes match the history of storytelling over time. Other great moments in history chronicle someone coming back from a trip to tell the story of where they had been that conveys new knowledge for many. For instance, French astronaut Jean-François Clervoy said in an interview in July 2020, "I thought it would be cool to see Earth from space, but I never thought it would be to the point that I would have tears." The emotional experience both embarrassed him and changed him. After all, "Astronauts are seen as tough guys who can control their emotions. You don't expect astronauts to tell others about being affected by their emotions." Clervoy went on to say, "From the moon, the earth looks so small and limited. It is on the background of a black sky that covers almost all your field of view. And there is nothing else around. And you love it. You have a feeling of love, like you love your partner, or your kids. You love looking at it. It's not only awe and admiration, it's the feeling of sensing a creator somewhere because it's too beautiful to be just by chance. And I think it's maybe more the feeling of love than the beauty that made my eyes get wet with tears."[14]

In June 2008, Ron Garan was at the International Space Station with his feet clamped onto the robotic Canadarm2 on a spacewalk. The

Canadarm2 arm can retrieve, repair, and deploy satellites and can be used as an inspection aid to allow the flight crew members to view the orbiter or payload surfaces through a television camera. While Garan was clamped onto it, the arm performed a maneuver known as the windshield wiper, taking him across a long arc above the space station and back.[15] He described his reaction this way: "As I approached the top of this arc, it was as if time stood still, and I was flooded with emotion and awareness. Here I was a hundred feet above the space station, looking down at this incredible man-made accomplishment against the backdrop of our indescribably beautiful Earth, 240 miles below. It was a deeply moving experience, for as I looked down at this stunning, fragile earth I saw it as an island that protects life from the harshness of space. And a sadness came over me. I was struck by an undeniable, sobering thought. I couldn't help but think of the inequity that exists on our apparent paradise. I couldn't help but think of all the people who don't have clean water to drink or enough food to eat, of the social injustices, conflicts, and poverty that remain pervasive through the Earth."[16]

The Overview Effect was reduced to one simple concept: a change in consciousness. And with that change came a heightened sense of empathy, which most astronauts referred to as "elevated empathy." From space, no one can see borders. Garan called it "just one Earth of a spaceship carrying us all to an unknown destination."[17] The cognitive shift gives a profound understanding of the interconnection of all life.

Astronaut Nicole Stoff noticed that there is only one border that matters—the thin blue line of atmosphere that blankets and protects us all.[18]

All the astronauts interviewed agreed that the silence, the feeling of weightlessness, and the blackness all played a part to send a message not just to space flyers but to all of humanity. They came back with the message that the future of Earth is to be shared. It is our home together. The view from orbit or the moon does not include divisions of race or class. Everyone must be a part of humanity's future evolution, not a privileged few.[19] In other words, when we save one another, we save ourselves.

Frank White says this realization leads to the need for a social contract, meaning we need to think back to what America's founders in the seventeenth century were facing: the essential question of how to guarantee rights and responsibilities for people without resorting to arms and war. Thomas Hobbes in his work *Leviathan* argues for the creation of a sovereign state because otherwise people would live in a constant state of war. Revered American architect of the 1900s Buckminster Fuller believed that social scientists needed to return to the "traditions of their forebears who supplied the foundations of political thinking"—meaning Jefferson, Franklin, and John Adams as they contemplated the best form of government for a new nation.[20] While our founders were dealing with this dilemma, they were aware that they were doing something that had never been done before. Turning away from thinking that all governments must be led by a king was a radical thought. It took guts, education, and a belief in goodness for our Founding Fathers to take it on.

No doubt setting a new nation on earth must have felt similar to floating in space. It was Abigail Adams who ardently worried about us women, grabbing the ear of her powerful husband to warn him: "Remember the Ladies." In a clever move to upend the apple cart carrying the belief that women should not own property—and even in most instances should be *viewed as property*—Abigail on her deathbed willed all her holdings to her granddaughters and nieces. Her husband called her "saucy." Goodness gracious, how I love John Adams!

Until my own Overview Effect kicked in, I

never would have searched out the intricacies of America's founding to try to understand who we are, to realize that we are all traveling in the same direction, that we are all hanging on to spaceship Earth—and that I should love those crowding my space, even those with whom I heartily disagree. Which, of course, led me to Thomas Jefferson.

*I could come home
after slings and arrows
of criticism, and there
would be Buddy,
keeping it simple.*

CHAPTER ELEVEN

The Agonies of Being a Writer

He loved words; he loved horses; he loved good food and gracious living. And like me, as a writer he had to endure criticism and calls for revisions, especially when he wrote the Declaration of Independence. Jefferson arrived in Philadelphia for the 1776 Congress at the age of thirty-three with a migraine headache. He wore the reputation of being an awesome wordsmith, which is why when a committee of five was tasked with coming up with a declaration to establish a new sovereign nation, he was a shoo-in.

With no shared ancestry or religion to hold together the hodgepodge of immigrants fleeing to British America to escape religious persecution or debtors' prison or to secure riches of land, the fact that Jefferson came up with the Declaration as our agent of connection is a stand-alone miracle. In essence, the Declaration brings an Overview Effect to us earthlings.

While he wrote "We hold these truths…" as the opening, he had in front of him George Mason's *Virginia's Declaration of Rights* that stated, "All men are born created equally free and independent and given certain inherent natural rights…among which are the enjoyment of liberty, with the means of acquiring and possessing property, and pursuing and obtaining happiness and safety."[21]

Lord have mercy! By the grace of Jefferson's pen, we escaped having a creed that reads like an insurance policy warning us that we are not covered for flood damage.

Since Jefferson was an accomplished musician, his love for music infused his pen. As an aside, which you are probably already thinking about, he believed that sex was the greatest human passion. In addition to Sally Hemings, history preserves several of his escapades when he was hotly pursuing even married women. Yep, he was a rascal. And while there is not much reason to have all this about Thomas Jefferson in a book about Buddy, I think everyone should review all this because essentially, Jefferson is us. If we list every personality trait in the human repertoire, he could have illustrated most of them— sour and sweet, brilliance, ego-driven stubbornness, vain, humble, passionate yet clueless. It was said that he never exhibited a temper except when his horse misbehaved. *Pardonnez-moi*, but I'm in love with the man. I would have even cooked him lasagna.

After his death, according to his first biographer who published his book about Jefferson's life in 1865, it was found that Jefferson had a secret drawer where he kept envelopes holding locks of hair of his dead wife and various other things of those he had loved. On each of the envelopes, he had written endearments, and the envelopes were all arranged in perfect order with signs of frequent handling.[22]

When his wife on her deathbed made him promise not to marry again so their children would not suffer the truncated parental love that she herself had suffered as a stepchild, there's no telling what that did to Jefferson. But the point is, Jefferson put both music and passion into his writing to give us a lovely idea, which we all know is not a reality. Yet the words "created equal" give us something to shoot for. The Declaration of Independence is essentially permission to dream.

While he and John Adams were writing the document together, and Jefferson was going through writers' hell answering criticisms that called for some *eighty* revisions, the two men formed a bond. They became so glued together while working toward the same goal, they became a living metaphor for the nation. Here was a Southern slaveholder and a New England Puritan farmer working together for the good of others. Their friendship was legendary. But as in all good stories, trouble was brewing.

When Jefferson and Adams became the second and third presidents, and the first of different parties to transfer power, their friendship broke apart. At the root of their dispute was their different beliefs in the role of government. Jefferson believed government should protect the people; Adams believed government should protect the people *from* themselves. Different political parties organized around these basic ideas, setting us on a path of constant struggle for compromise and balance.

After Jefferson and Adams as presidents exchanged power, they were so pissed off at each other, they did not write or speak to each other for the next twelve years. This bothered one founder more than all the others, and he is the one who also captures my heart: Benjamin Rush.

He was a physician who had just turned thirty when he got himself elected to the 1776 Congress.

He was drawn to politics partly because he wanted to prevent slavery from becoming part of the new nation as it was being formed. But he was a terrible politician. He had a hard time keeping his mouth shut. He thought he knew what was best for everyone and insisted on his ideas in an almost nonstop discourse. He was almost always right, of course, and since he had a photographic memory, he could back up his points. He saw people suffering and he wanted to help them. As soon as he signed the Declaration of Independence, he rode off to take care of the troops on the battlefield in the Revolutionary War.[23]

When he saw the terrible conditions that the soldiers had to put up with—lack of medical supplies and more soldiers dying from disease in hospitals than in battle—he turned on George Washington and tried to get him fired as the commander of the army.

It turned out that Rush was so much of a gadfly when the Constitutional Congress was formed to write a constitution, he was not allowed to be in the room. By then, he had made up with George Washington and started inviting the great man to supper at his Philadelphia home, where he would talk nonstop while Washington was eating. Rush's wild-hearted dedication to trying to improve everyone's plight never lessened.

Indeed, physicians live life on a different level, which I know about from being married to one. I think of doctors as being like a pit stop in an auto race. Drivers pull off for a tire change or a can of oil, and then get back onto the raceway. Dr. Rush did what he could to keep everyone in the race, but he was sorely hampered by scientific ignorance at the time. When someone had an illness, doctors in the 1700s often thought that their patients were possessed by demons. Though breaking from this view, Rush didn't have much to replace it. He had no alternative, either, against following the next dogma: believing that all diseases were carried in the blood. Hence, he bled his patients, sometimes unintentionally to death.

Every day, he trudged into poor neighborhoods, stepping over sewage to treat the ill who lined up hoping to receive relief. He would coo, *There now, we'll fix that. You won't hurt much longer.* His main treatment was improving his patients' hygiene and nutrition, which often seemed as if he'd performed a miracle. It was the only thing he knew he could do.

It was at the 1776 Congress when Rush, Jefferson, and Adams took breaks together at the Schuylkill River that they formed a dedicated friendship. They were all so classically educated, they could talk on any subject. Young and optimistic, they stayed in touch after the founding congresses set a new nation on the globe. And when the Jefferson–Adams friendship shattered, Rush saw the dissolution as a danger. After all, John Adams and Jefferson were a living metaphor for the nation.

Their estrangement suggested that the nation itself might also break apart.

One day, in his old age, Adams wrote Rush that he thought he should say goodbye to Jefferson while there was still time. Rush jumped at the chance. This was just what he'd been hoping for—the opening to reconnect them all. He wrote both Adams and Jefferson, and kept at it, telling Jefferson what Adams said about him, then relaying that thought back to Adams. He kept gently cajoling the two old founders to reach out to each other.

Adams wrote Rush, *Tell Jefferson that I will always love him.* When Rush conveyed the message to Jefferson, a rich correspondence opened between the two, fueled at first by their worrying who would be alive to tell the story of the Founders. Their shared memories led to an outpouring of letters. In fact, in the last fourteen years of their lives, Jefferson and Adams exchanged over one hundred long letters. Thoughts flew back and forth between them, agreeing on their astonishing optimism in thinking they could bring forth a new nation on earth made up of a diverse group of people who could want the best for one another and govern with that in mind. In the last days of their lives, John Adams, having lost his hearing and losing his eyesight and grumpy as hell, wrote Jefferson, "While I breathe, I shall be your friend."[24]

Benjamin Rush's skill in healing Jefferson and Adams's friendship is a riveting, valuable study. But for another important thought, Jefferson, more than any other Founder, personifies the irony of America by being a slaveowner at the same time he was writing one of the most inspiring documents in human history. And get this: When his beloved Monticello fell into disrepair, a Jewish family bought it to restore it in appreciation of Jefferson's having written into the Virginia Constitution a guarantee for religious freedom.

For the rest of his life, Jefferson griped about

those requested revisions in his Declaration of Independence. Even until the day he died, he insisted that his original draft had been mangled.

Luckily with Buddy, there were no such complications. I could come home after slings and arrows of criticism, and there would be Buddy, keeping it simple. To quote the great poet Robert Frost, *Home is the place where, when you have to go there, they have to take you in.* For Buddy and me, though, *home* meant more than a location held in place by a birth certificate. I was not a good driver. I was not a good cook. I suffered from bouts of assholism. Yet Buddy had chosen me.

Oh, by the way, do you remember that Jefferson and Adams died on the same day? And to make that even stranger, that day was July 4, the fiftieth anniversary of the nation they helped found? Not many stranger things have happened. And the magic is that you can give that fact any meaning you want. That's the beauty of metaphors.

*I finally learned that
if I was going to boss
someone around to
improve them, the desire
for improvement had to
come from within them,
not from me.*

CHAPTER TWELVE

All I Need to Know about AI, I Learned from My Dog

When I went to college, I majored in psychology. I worked in the mental health field for a while. As base as it sounds, I had two reasons: I wanted to write novels and create compelling characters, so seeing a wide variety of people, including those who were troubled and even those who were certified nuts, would be to my advantage as a writer. And I wanted to diagnose everyone in my family.

It should have been that I simply wanted to help people who were having a hard time. But my empathy muscle then was not at the level of an Overview Effect.

I learned, however, that anger is a form of self-medication for depression. A surefire way to get a severely depressed human to move is to fire up their anger. That is a quick way to reconnect them to living. As we all know, there're plenty of things to be vexed about. As a starter, you can try the weather—it's never just right. I used to have a T-shirt that read, "The more you complain, the longer God lets you live." I know a lot of people who are testing that theory, apparently planning on living a long, long time, which, of course, will give them more time to complain.

Today, all sorts of drugs can assist in taking an off-ramp from depression. But from my old-time view, you could say we live in a world today made up of people who are self-medicating their depression with anger.

One of my friends, who was the former mayor of our little city, told me that she took her child to parents' night at school years after she had stepped down from office. Yet there at her child's school, a man came up to her and doused her with a bucket of anger, pouring his wrath over her for something she had done years ago. Understandably, she was wounded and confused. How, she wondered, could she still be the target of such a rant? When I suggested what I knew from working in mental health—that her assailant was likely driven by depression—she said, "Ah." Understanding that released her from taking his rant personally. Which leads us to the next big question: How can we keep so many from becoming so depressed that they become addicted to anger?

The most tried-and-true method is what Elie Wiesel said in his Nobel lecture in 1986: *Just as despair can come to one only from other human beings, hope, too, can be given to one only by other human beings.*

What a beautiful sentiment. We can treat one another! We don't need a PhD or a medical degree!

I had only to remember back to the image of Buddy lying in the street—not moving, curled up, seemingly barely alive until you got out of your car to check if he was breathing—and learning that the root of his sadness was that he didn't have anyone to own. He'd been genetically hardwired to guard someone, to worry about someone. The cure was that I gave him a home in the same sense that the astronauts experienced the Overview Effect. To Buddy, I *was* home.

There was something else too. It had been clear to my family that I was born with a dash of hot sauce in my genome. My grandmother often said, "Little Shelley is going to kill us all." She said it with affection, for I was always embroiling her in one of my schemes.

Back when I was five, living in Hot Springs, Arkansas, because my father was helping to construct a dam—which gave me the perfect opportunity to tell everyone we had moved there for some dam business—I pushed even my father into wanting to do something to give the family a few hours of peace without me. He paid—he actually *paid*—for me to go to a private kindergarten, since in those days, there were no public kindergartens. You started school at the age of six, cold turkey. There was no preparation other than your family telling you to sit down and shut up. Not literally, of course, but it was rather similar to training a puppy.

Right away in that private kindergarten, I learned every kid's name and weakness, such as who was a scaredy-cat and who was a bully. I made each five-year-old ask me for permission at recess to use the swing, to get in the sandbox, and to get on the teeter-totter, where they could act out their empathy or apathy by holding someone in the air until the other person begged for mercy. I admit that I was not only this much of a dictator but also that I sat on the teeter-totter holding someone in the air until they agreed that I could be their dictator for life. (I exaggerate here, but Lord, it's in the service of giving you exercise by laughing. And if you ain't laughing, another chance is coming in the next chapter.)

Funny how those two words, apathy and empathy, are so much alike. For someone like me who was willing to sacrifice exact meaning for the love of a rhyme, who embraced the word *turd* before I knew what it meant, mixing up *apathy* for *empathy* was a natural failing. In time, I was forced to confront my apathy by becoming a parent. You see, my inclination to be bossy followed me into adulthood. I especially loved being a mother because in the early years of motherhood, I was in total control (at least for the most part) of my children's lives. Only a top-notch tantrum would challenge my position as generalissimo. And even then, I could walk away and trigger my toddlers' separation anxiety so they'd come running, screaming after me.

My comeuppance came when my kids were teenagers. I finally learned that if I was going to boss someone around to improve them, the desire for improvement had to come from within *them*, not from me. In short, I think mothers give birth to children so we can be humbled. Nothing teaches you humility more quickly than learning you are not the be-all and end-all to someone when they reach the age of eighteen. It's time then to settle down to being the wind beneath their wings as they leave home and establish their own lives.

This brings me back to Buddy, who every day was acting as my security guard as if I were a pop star. Certainly, he was instinctively drawn to my pack-leader aura that had allowed me to be a kindergarten dictator. And, get this, it was in that kindergarten that I first fell in love. It happened at juice time. His name was Billy Bundy. (And Billy, if you're still alive, I still love you.)

Ah, men. I realized early on that nothing could send me into a state of excitement and well-being more than the sound of my name in a male voice giving me compliments, genuine and heartfelt. And still does. Such as the words that John Adams in Philadelphia at the 1776 Congress wrote to his wife, Abigail, back in Boston, separated by four hundred miles, even as their letters were threatened by British spies capturing them and making them public. John Adams didn't give a hoot if anyone stole his words and broadcast his private thoughts about the '76 Congress: "It is like a large fleet sailing under convoy. The fleetest sailors must wait for the dullest and slowest. I fear that in every assembly, members will obtain an influence by noise not sense. By meanness, not greatness. By ignorance not learning. By contracted hearts, not large souls...."[25] And what he said to Abigail, his beloved wife, is what every wife wants to hear: "Is there no way for two friendly souls to converse together, 400 miles off? Yes, by letter. But I want to hear you think, or to see your thoughts. You bid me burn your letters. But I must forget you first." And then he reminded her, "I think you shine as a stateswoman."[26]Always he made her feel that he could do nothing without her. And so there you have it, the essential feeling all women want from men.

The fact that there is absolutely no one else on the planet like a good-hearted man is perhaps best expressed by female blues singers. As for today when so many men have changed our lives through their proclivity for inventing things, I have a new fear. Of course women have participated in this, too, for computer whizzes are not limited to one gender. I fear the uncertainty of what artificial intelligence will do to us. Already, I feel as if I'm living in a fun house—you know, one of those carnival attractions where you go in to see yourself in a mirror that distorts every part of you. The Internet can do this now too. Indeed, our fun house has moved to our phones. Your face is pulled wide; your nose is smashed. You look like yourself only enough to recognize yourself; otherwise, your every feature appears blurred. Our everyday selves have vanished. To bring ourselves back, we have to work hard to remind ourselves that what we see in that mirror is not really us but a distorted version of ourselves.

When I think back about how Buddy knew I could be his pack leader and yet let him do his job in protecting me, I assume he was using senses I do not have. They say that a dog can sense cancers. They can detect an oncoming seizure. They can tell when someone does not like them.

In this new technological age that warns me that I will be living in a fun house with all the lines blurred between reality and delusion, we will have to sniff out reality. We'll have to develop senses we do not yet know we have. We'll have to sense what is real and good. We'll have to use whatever proof we can find, much like using the scientific method that is self-correcting. The fact that Buddy saw me come out of the house every morning to head to the barn to feed my horses, to plant a lipstick kiss on him and each horse, the fact that I was home all day writing some book or other, gave him a reality he could count on. But darn, I miss my phone book where I can touch the page of the name, address, and phone number of any earthling I want to reach.

On that note, when our world seems now to be spinning at a new rate, agreeing on what reality is will be a challenge. It will be a central concern in our next chapter on this earth. We will either solve it or else give up on it, and just go with the flow. I remember a piece of information I came upon when I did that deep dive into our founding history. I took on that study when so much division and infighting in our nation was hampering my ready-to-laugh at most anything. I wanted to know who we Americans were when we first started out and had we changed? In my research, I found one of the most humorous and disturbing facts that related to our new world of AI.

When the British king levied the Stamp Act on his American colony, the law demanded that our ancestors buy a stamp to put on legal documents, as well as a bunch of other stuff, even on playing cards. It became a main reason for America to break from King George III. And to create a bit of sympathy for George, remember he was green and dumb about human nature. He saw his American colony as a gravy train to pay off his war debts. It was the Stamp Act that sent the colonists over the edge, even inspiring Patrick Henry to bark: *Give me liberty or give me death!*

The objection to the tax was so ferocious that King George nullified it after only one year, but the damage had been done. Grievance against the tax had taken on a life of its own. An illogical fear entered the mainstream, so much so that one night when a farmer told his servant to go check on the livestock in the barn, the servant trembled, refusing, saying the Stamp Act might be out there.[27]

* * *

If a Stamp Act can help fuel a revolution by taking on human traits, artificial intelligence will put voices in our heads. We will have to develop the discriminating power of a dog's nose to sniff out what is tricking us.

Italian theoretical physicist and writer Carlo Rovelli has this wonderful joke about identifying reality. Two men are arguing. The first says, "You are in the right." The second insists, "You're also right." The first man's wife, who is overhearing in the next room, yells out: "You can't both be in the right!" The first man nods and says to her, "And you're right too."

Rovelli defines reality as not things but connections. "Quantum mechanics have taught us that the world is a continuous, restless swarming of things…a world of happenings, not of things. Our reality is tears and laughter, gratitude, altruism, and loyalty and betrayal." Rovelli even encourages me to apply quantum mechanics to Buddy and me: "our emotions, our loves, are no less real for being shared with the animal world."[28] As an important voice in modern physics, Rovelli gives a knife-stab warning. "We are perhaps the only species on Earth to be conscious of the inevitability of our individual mortality. I fear that soon we will knowingly watch its own collective demise, or at least the demise of its civilization....The brutal climate and environmental changes we have triggered are unlikely to spare us... especially since public and political opinion prefers to ignore the dangers that we are running, hiding our heads in the sand."[29]

But most of all, Rovelli says, "We understand the world not as made by things but by kisses."[30] Once given, poof! A kiss is gone except for the feeling it leaves. Certainly Buddy understood that. Every morning the branding of my kiss on his forehead—until it faded or was wiped off by his running through brush, or tall weeds, or by the sudden downpour of a summer rain—was Buddy's and my reality; it was all we needed to say to each other.

When you know the
essence of someone—
not their outside version
but their inside version—
all physical differences
disappear.

CHAPTER THIRTEEN

Verna Mae and I Mess with the World

In 1950 when I was six, a polio epidemic blew through the Mississippi River Delta. It swept me up as the only kid in our town to be swatted down. This was a serious detour in my life, for I was immediately driven to an isolation hospital in Memphis. There, contagious to the public, I was put in a ward with many other children, lying in beds wall-to-wall. That year, thirty-three thousand other children across the nation were stricken with the poliovirus, which today few people know about. But what I want to tell you is this: While I was separated from the public, isolated from my family, my mother stood outside the ward window waving at me. She wore a tweed suit and a broad-brim hat, looking like the movie star she craved to be. I made hand signals to her for what I needed. First was a cup of coffee. No nurse would allow a six-year-old to have coffee. Oh good heavens! My mother finally finagled sending me in a thermos of half-cream, half-coffee, and the world became brighter. Then the mail started coming.

Everyone in my first-grade class sent me a get-well card or letter. But the most magical piece of mail that arrived that day was a letter from Verna Mae. When I opened it up, written across the top was HOLD THIS UP TO A MIRROR. I spent all afternoon puzzling out the words that Verna Mae had written backward. Think about that: shut up in a ward all day before the days of TV, there was little for us kids to do to kill the boredom. And think about how clever you'd have to be to write a whole letter backward! I couldn't do that today even if the prize were a wheelbarrow of Milk Duds.

But as my days in that isolation hospital were counted out over the next three months, I experienced an awakening as soul-changing as going into space. When two children died near me, I realized my life had been saved. The dreaded iron lung had not had to be plugged in. I could breathe; I could move. A few muscles had been lost, but that is minor compared to not being able to breathe.

Every week Verna Mae sent me letters written backward. Most often they were jokes. *How do you know an elephant is in the bed with you? You smell the peanuts on his breath.* She sent news like the modern-day Twitter/X feed: *Two chickens fried for your grandmother's club meeting. The school band's cake walk Saturday. Mrs. Raynor's cat got in her chicken yard. You are missed. Always remember, You are loved. Verna.*

When those two kids died near me, the Overview Effect kicked in. At my age, I was still in the phase of magical thinking, which began editing what had happened to me. I said to myself, *I'm being saved for something.*

Saved! Yes, saved!

I would not be leaving the earth, at least not that day or anytime soon. And then the next question came as logically as a constant in an algebra problem: *But for what? What am I being saved for?* Frankly, that's a good question for everyone to ask. You don't even have to have a brush with death to ask it. *What am I being saved for?*

Years later my mother and I talked about that moment. She said she prayed all night asking the Lord to spare me. And when she started that sentence, "I promised the Lord…" I stopped her. "Don't tell me." I was afraid she'd promised I'd cure cancer or, at least, ingrown toenails. Or become the first female pope, which would really be hard because we weren't Catholic. But all along, I knew the answer for myself. When I was five years old, I'd already decided what I was intended to be. I was saved to write books, to put words together to give pleasure to readers, to comfort, to connect with those who would be enlightened by the power of story and the joy of words.

After three months, I was let out of the isolation hospital, and when my mother had to drive me back weekly for physical therapy sessions, she used that time for shopping in the big city. She would bring Verna Mae along to take my wheelchair out of the station wagon. Verna usually wore a white maid's uniform, and she would push me around while my mother tried on dresses and looked for a new purse.

One day, a man and woman stared at me, took in the fact of Verna in charge of my wheels, and came over and said, "You poor little thing," then dropped a handful of coins in the starched lap of my dress.

"Ice cream time," Verna sang and wheeled a U-turn to whiz me out the door.

That was over seventy years ago now. But Verna and I both remember that day the same. When I call her now in the nursing home where she has been the last few years, and we mention that day, she asks, "Did you have strawberry or vanilla?" "Chocolate," I say.

I can walk now, if not well, and she can still finish my sentences, practicing her smarts the same way she did when I was a child. In the 1960s civil rights era, she became a town commissioner, a newspaper columnist, and helped Bill Clinton organize the Arkansas African American vote. When we talk about the day of the quick U-turn, though, we remember it exactly the same, but never put words to how it made each of us feel. We know only that we understand it the same. We still enjoy playing with the idea that we passed up a chance to become rich. By wearing braces and using crutches or a wheelchair I could have held up a pity Mason jar for people to drop money into and likely made enough money to pay my family's and Verna's electric bills for months. Verna Mae and I laugh, matching our senses of humor, loving our shared memories that are like diamonds we wear only in private.

In thinking about how we each can get a life blow—which the character of Jody in Marjorie Kinnan Rawlings's masterpiece, *The Yearling*, taught us to think of as "getting our share"—we should stay open to revision. For instance, a related illumination came to me only recently. Several friends invited me to lunch to tell me they each were dealing with a body problem. One needed a new hip, another two new knees, one a new kidney. I was eating along as I usually do, talking with my mouth half full, squeezing the bread to see how fresh it was, when all of a sudden I realized they had sought me out because they thought of me as physically different, as *disabled*. And they wanted comfort and guidance.

These words—disabled, handicapped, crippled—are so wrong for anyone. Furthermore, these words have never entered my mind in relation to me. My identity is beyond that. When you know the essence of someone—not their outside version but their inside version—all physical differences disappear. Like Faulkner said in *The Reivers*—which, by the way, everyone should read the book or see the film—"Our outsides were only what we lived in and slept in, our insides were what we really were."[31] In other words, the body is only the vessel for the soul.

I guess here would be a good place to share my Faulkner story. For you see, when it was time for me to go to college, I chose to head to the University of Mississippi. I knew Faulkner lived near the campus and that he'd won the Nobel Prize for literature. I figured he knew something about writing. I wanted him to teach me. I wrote him a letter to tell him I was coming. I addressed it *William Faulkner, Oxford, Mississippi.* In those little towns, the postmaster knew everyone so I knew he'd get it. But then shortly before I arrived, he died. I took it personally. It seemed he'd gone to great lengths to avoid me.

I bucked up and signed up to study writing anywhere that would let me in. I also became an autodidact, one of those fancy words that means I started figuring things out on my own. Besides, I've partly wanted to write things that would get back at ol' Tennessee Williams for making that girl in *The Glass Menagerie* so pitiful she can't get a boyfriend. That play is an insult to men. Here we had a girl who limped, who lived in a fantasy world, and her brother and mother viewed her as a burden. They thought if they could only get her married off, they'd be set free. Baloney! The girl wasn't their problem. Case in point: one night at one of my dinner parties, a young surgical resident lamented that he couldn't find a woman to marry. I coaxed him out until he finally explained, "I need someone with a few tire treads on her. I want to spend my life with someone who has experienced enough knocks that she knows what matters."

Which brings me to the subject of drugs. And wasted time. When I had corrective surgery in my teens to get the most out of the muscles that had not been paralyzed by the poliovirus, I was nearly addicted to morphine. Floating away into space was oh so deliciously tempting. No more worries. No more challenges. I could just float on out, letting everyone else worry about feeding me and bathing me and buying my cookies and paying for my hair upkeep.

But once you've answered that question— *What am I being saved for?*—you can't take a vacation via drugs or alcohol. I embrace every discomfort, every anxiety, every bad day—even those that unleash a rhyming list of cusswords— as moments not to be missed. Life is so short, you have to "hop to it."

I know it's said that history doesn't repeat

itself, it only rhymes, but facts are facts, and here's one that's a knife-stab. It's a cautionary tale as to the subject of physical differences and the fact that we are a world of different shades and talents and that with my physical difference wrought by a virus, I could have been waiting in a line in Germany in 1940. That was the year Hitler and his dumbass crew came up with T4, a plan to euthanize disabled children in their pursuit of the racially pure society. The name T4 came from the street address of the program.[32]

I now qualify for a parking sticker that lets me put my car in the choicest spot closest to where I'm going, so everyone wants to ride with me. Following the wisdom of the folk saying, "When you're in the donkey's house, don't talk about ears," I'm going to put a plaque on my dashboard reading: "When you're in this car, don't talk about my driving." And that would even apply to Buddy if he were still here. But then, of course he thought everything I did was the most wonderful thing he'd ever seen.

* * *

Verna Mae is now ninety-four years old, living in the nursing home in the little cotton town that I love. It is also the nursing home where my mother lived when she was nearly ninety. A lifetime of smoking had taken its toll on her. She slipped into dementia, which made her funnier in some ways, sadder in others. But before I begin another story, know this: Hard knocks are handed out to all of us in a random fashion. It's gumption that can be learned.

Now when I call Verna Mae in the same nursing home in my beloved Arkansas town where my mother died, Verna Mae answers my call with, "Hello, sweet girl." And she always hangs up with, "Know you are loved."

Turning to my favorite kind of story, the kind that is always a winner, take note. They are in abundance around us.

It's been said that God
gave us memory
so that we might have
roses in December.

CHAPTER FOURTEEN

Dumb Crooks

My husband told me about a young man, one of his shiftless boyhood friends, who went fishing every chance he got. Stopping at the bait shop on his way to the river, he filched a fishing rod. Let's call it "having sticky fingers." But the twist was that he caught such a big fish that a photographer from the newspaper heard about it and rushed to take his picture for that week's sports page. There the sticky-fingered fisherman was posing straight up and still, holding his filched fishing rod. No need to say, when the cops saw the photo, they were on it. Three weeks in jail, a hefty fine, and no fishing for a month.

To do my part in controlling the population of dumb crooks, I once gave this assignment in a writing workshop to answer the question, "Why

I'm Afraid I'm Going to Hell as a Dumb Crook."
I like to oil students' memories of their childhoods
during that time when they developed a conscience.
Living with the guilt of doing something that was
not really serious but what they thought could send
them to eternal damnation adds up to priceless
subject matter for a writer—like the day the teacher
gives you sharp scissors instead of those blunt ones.
And you just can't help it; you snip off the pigtail of
a girl sitting close to you.

A young man in my writing workshop wrote
such a good piece carved from his own life that he
got it published. He was from a little rural town
where the school's field trip was to visit a prison.
(Holy guacamole, how I love America! Where else
would a fifth-grade field trip be planned to visit
the state prison?) My student described in hilarious detail the food he'd been served in that prison
cafeteria and decided it was so awful, he would
never do anything to get sent there as an inmate.

My own story of dealing with dumb crooks started soon after my mother had to move to the nursing home in the little Arkansas town I love. She craved having someone to sit with her, not only to ease her loneliness but also to provide a steady audience for her ongoing comedy routines, which became even funnier as she lost her marbles. Since I live in Florida, miles away from the Arkansas town where my mother was happy in the nursing home, where everyone still knew her and visited, I sent the word out that I was looking for sitters to be with her, to feed her, to dress her, and to keep her company.

Calls started coming in the rhythm of tele-marketers. I finally hired a mother–daughter duo who said they would tag team throughout the day and night sitting with my mother. Then other calls starting coming with hysterical voices, "Shelley, you've hired streetwalkers to sit with your mother!"

Well, I couldn't fire them based on hearsay. My sweet side thought they wanted to improve their lot in life. After all, the daughter of the duo had a two-year-old child. I flew up there to see for myself. When I walked into my mother's room, she was dressed in a see-through pink blouse with tons of ruffles and was wearing enough makeup to give Tammy Faye Baker a run for her money. Most of all, my mother loved it. She was smiling and welcoming, and I tabled the idea of firing the sitters.

But then they started charging me for days they did not come. And then they began to call to say my check had been lost in the mail. They even gave me the postmaster's phone number to back them up. I didn't try. I figured he was in on the scheme. I wrote them a nice letter saying they were the best sitters my mother had ever had, but that my mother decided she didn't need them right now, and maybe we'd get back to them later. I figured flattering crooks is necessary to keep them from retaliating, and I didn't want my mother to be mistreated in any way. But I have to admit my conscience still bothers me from telling that white lie stained with self-interest.

I next hired a woman named Hilda. She was one of the loveliest people I have ever known. And the poorest. She had grown up as one of ten kids picking cotton until she reached the eighth grade, then dropped out of school to work full-time. She married, and she and her husband went to Michigan where he worked in a car factory. When he died, she came back to live where she'd grown up. And get this: she was a year older than my mother—eighty-five going on eighty-six.

Every week, Hilda and I would talk on the phone. She would tell me what my mother had done, and we talked to each other like close family. She was my mainstay for several years until she called me one night starting with, "I have bad news," then added, "no, it's not about your mother. It's just that I went to the doctor today and he told me I have the beginning stages of Alzheimer's."

Before I had fully comprehended what she had said, my mouth opened and this flew out: "Just forget what he said and keep coming." She did for a while, and every day I had a moment of prayer for her driving skills to hold on.

Shortly after, Hilda moved into the nursing home down the hall from my mother. They died a few days apart.

Since we're on this subject, I'll add a story I told on national radio that became a favorite. But today it troubles me. You see, I made it sweet, too sweet, and now that I have lived so long I know I overdid it. When two of my closest friends came to tell me that they each had been diagnosed with that brain disease that steals memories, they wept and worried about how it would affect their families. Quick to offer comfort, I said, "But then we'll have a chance to perform acts of love."

Ah yes. That's true. But it also leaves out sorrow and the exhaustion that goes with it.

My radio essay had been drawn from a day I was shopping in the grocery store when a man ran down the aisle and grabbed me, crying out, "Well looky here who I've found! I'm so glad to see you!"

I looked into his face and hugged him back and said that I was so very glad to see him too. And then I waited for his name to come to me.

This was the grocery store where I used to roll a cart holding my son wearing diapers after I picked him up from nursery school. I always got him a fried chicken leg to suck on to keep him busy while I tried to remember all I needed for the next week's recipes. But on that day when that man was giving me a bear hug, my son had already grown up and moved out. Yet in that grocery store, I often saw people I'd known over all those years. They would call out, "How's your son? Does he still like chicken legs?" "Yes," I'd call back, "and he no longer wears diapers."

On that day when that man's face was so full of joy in seeing me, I was sure he and I had once been very special to each other. Had he been my son's second-grade teacher who so warmly reassured me that no, I had not ruined my son by teaching him how to play craps as the best way I knew for him to practice addition tables? Or could he be the man who promised not to tell anybody when he found me at a mother–son picnic beating the fishing worms to death because I couldn't stand to put them on the hooks *wiggling*?

Then a woman, who was apparently this man's wife, touched my arm and apologized. "He thinks he knows you," she whispered. She took him by the hand to coax him away, glancing back with the embarrassment of one who cares for someone whose memory has been misaligned by the disease that is usually accompanied by age. I was sorry she was embarrassed because I was still savoring being the object of his joyful greeting.

My face must have jiggled loose the memory of someone very special in his past. And I was more than happy to be whomever he wanted me to be. Besides, my own memories were making up parts for him in my life too.

It's been said that God gave us memory so that we might have roses in December. And ol' Tennessee Williams—who really has written some good stuff—gave us the quote that in memory everything seems to happen to music. Well, in the grocery store that day, I had one of my finest moments. I was a rose dancing in a memory.

There it was —
a realization about
my own life and the
serenity I could gain
in accepting it for just
what it was: a ride of
uncertain destination.

CHAPTER FIFTEEN

Taking Stock

We had been living on our farm for years now. Skip was happy. He still didn't sweat, but with several fans in his stall and cool showers, I kept him comfortable. And he was getting old. There was no way I could prevent that.

Then I began to feel the rumblings of dreams beyond reach, awakening a gnawing to fulfill some of my life's aspirations. I wanted to ride in a national championship. I wanted to do something huge like that. I wanted to feel cool. Some people want to run marathons or break up a marriage to feel the excitement of finding someone again. But here I was wanting to do something that could be labeled loopy or silly. I wanted to compete in a really big horse show, and while I began telling people that I didn't want to win but just to *participate,* the truth was, I wanted to win the whole honkin' thing: a trophy, a blue ribbon, a medal. I even wanted to be the rodeo queen.

I had actually bought Skip at a horse show. On a day when no one at home or anywhere else needed me, I went to a local 4-H horse show where I sat in the arena all afternoon watching the horses and their riders go round and round. Sometimes they moved together; sometimes they bounced against each other resembling microwave popcorn banging the sides of its bag. And then they'd usually settle down.

As I watched them, I suddenly knew what it is that makes me so passionate about horses. It's not only their obvious beauty and grace and stoicism. Whenever I've read anything written about them, such as the beautiful passages by Cormac McCarthy in which he describes man's attraction to them because of their *ardentheartedness,* what he calls *the heat of the blood that ran them,* I know what I feel for them is quite a bit less refined yet no less spiritual. For as I sat in the arena that day, watching all of those horses going round and round, sweating, working something fierce to do whatever the people on their backs were asking them to do, I realized that not one of those horses knew where it was going. Instead, each had placed all of its belief that whoever was on its back *did* know. I also knew the human sitting up there didn't—not really. The people riding were going round and round, enjoying it but doing so because someone had made them believe it was something they should do. There it was—a realization about my own life and the serenity I could gain in accepting it for just what it was: a ride of uncertain destination.

When number seventeen came into the arena, I noticed how slow he was going. A flea-bitten grey with a teenager on his back. He was going so slow that his front leg had barely swung out of the way before his back leg came up to claim the dirt where it had been. But when the commands came out over the microphone, he got himself going pretty good. Then right after he lined up in front of the judge, he fell asleep.

This might be a horse I can ride, I thought. When he was announced as having won second place over a handful of others, and that he was up for sale, I followed him out of the arena. I stood for a while on the other side of the show grounds so I could just look over at him. He was standing in a huddle with some others near a corral. He still had that teenager on his back. Right away I felt a connection.

And I bought him. As soon as I got him settled in a stall where I boarded him, I swear I heard him sigh because he knew I would never want to go as fast as that teenager. Furthermore, he clearly read my heart. I'd been waiting for him all my life.

When the desire to do the wild thing of riding in a national championship hit me, it took some self-convincing. *As if I had good sense,* I could hear my father saying. *Being foolish with your money.* By then I had sold my second novel, *Replacing Dad,* to the movies. I was not taking money from my children's college funds, nor a family fund, but only from my own purse. I shouldn't feel guilty at all.

The problem was that Skip was not at that level. I needed a new horse, a competitive horse.

The other horse I owned living on the farm was the palomino I'd named Robert Redford. When I took him to a horse show, he flipped out. He'd been shown too much. His mind was fried. He bucked and fidgeted. He wanted to go home. I kept warning him that if he didn't straighten up, I was going to sell him down the river. Then the day he scared me beyond words, I jumped off and yelled, "That's it. I *am* selling you down the river."

Suddenly I felt as if I had just been zapped by a cattle prod. From deep in my subconscious, I had uttered words that I realized had come from a ton of phrases from growing up in the Mississippi Delta, where the days of slavery wrapped themselves around the tongues of white people, sharing a language that grew up between us. I remembered that when my mother cooked meals with Verna Mae working together in the kitchen for a Thanksgiving meal, my mother would dip a finger into a pie and exclaim, "It's larrupin' good."

Larrupin' good. That was a strange enough description that I wanted to look it up. Furthermore, there were so many more, such as when I was baffled and said, "I have no cotton-picking idea." And the songs. Oh the songs! We sing songs from slavery days that we don't even realize are slavery songs, like "Oh! Susanna," which a slave man wrote to sing to his sweetheart when he was sold away from her. Also "Michael, Row Your Boat Ashore," which slave men sang when they were rowing against a strong current to keep their oars in the same rhythm.

When I read the slave narratives collected by

writers in the days of the Great Depression, I found "larrupin' good" used by the young boy owned by Jefferson Davis. Essentially *larrupin' good* is a superb example of onomatopoeia—sounding just like what it means.

There are many other traces of how our American culture is soaked in slavery history, such as what Mississippi writer Eudora Welty wrote about in her collection of photographs, *One Time, One Place*, published in March 1971. She made a visual record of rural America during the Depression. Her experiences became the gristmill for her short stories and novels that earned awards throughout her life. Although Eudora Welty was not collecting ex-slave voices, she surely must have captured the photographs of some who had been born into slavery, and her feeling for those Africans seeps clearly through the words in her preface to her collection of photographs. As the reader looks at the photo of an old woman as the frontispiece,

Welty writes: *When a heroic face like that of the woman in the buttoned sweater looks back at me from her picture, what I respond to now, just as I did the first time, is not the Depression, not the Black, not the South, not even the perennially sorry state of the whole world, but the story of her life in her face. Her face to me is full of meaning more truthful and more terrible and, I think, more noble than any generalization about people could have prepared me for or could describe for me now. I learned from my own pictures, one by one, and had to; for I think we were the breakers of our own hearts.*[33]

What a rich culture we miss by not seeing how slave history and white history are intertwined! In my opinion, I wish we could read the full history of slavery, then see how we worked to correct it. And are still working to right our wrongs.

* * *

When my dream of riding in a national championship bumped into that problem of the big palomino who would rather kill me than ride me around in a big arena, I sold him and cried. He left many marks of his days at the farm, such as the one when he got cast in his stall, meaning he lay down too close to a wall and couldn't get his legs under him to get up—so he was stuck. Sometimes cowboys have to tie a rope to one of a cast horse's back legs to pull it over, but I was alone at the farm, so I improvised. I sang "Oh! Susanna" until Robert Redford figured it out for himself. But he thrashed around enough to break the stall door. Since my husband was busy and I didn't know how to fix it, I put it back together with Gorilla Glue. I performed enough of those similar miracles that I thought about changing the name of Blueberry Hill Farm to Gorilla Glue Ranch.

The dream of riding in a national championship did not wane, so on the spur of the moment, I flew out to Oklahoma, and with a trainer's help, bought myself an Appaloosa, vowing to take her back there the following year and ride her in the show myself. I bought a mare because I figured if she went lame, she could still have babies. Yes, females' fertility can always be of marketable value.

As a get-ready plan, I thought I should ride Skip in a few local shows to figure this thing out. I took a hardy supply of Gatorade to keep Skip from becoming overheated and dehydrated. He loved the orange flavor, but it made his lips a bit orange, giving him a weird look. But weird has never bothered me.

The first weekend that we went to a show, the judge was named Buck and he gave me and Skip fourth place. For the next show, the judge was named Goose. I put on diamond earrings the size of golf balls to set off my white Resistol cowboy hat. I wore black chaps and painted my fingernails Watermelon Pink to look nice holding the reins. Goose gave me first place. It was clear, he liked his women trashy. But then at the next shows I went to, Skip and I suddenly began coming in last. It took me a while to figure out the trouble: Neither he nor I could hold in our stomachs any longer.

We both went on diets. I kept him in his stall limiting his time to graze. I myself went on tomato juice and Ritz crackers five times a day. By the end of the week, neither he nor I looked much better and both of us were mean. We didn't even like each other much.

He became hard to catch, bringing back my memories of Nell. When I got close to him in the pasture, I reminded him that I was hungry enough to eat a horse. The end of this episode of training to ride in a national championship came down to this: I hid a box of sugar lumps in the tack room. When Skip and I got back from a ride, I'd pull one out and we'd each suck it like there was no tomorrow until the desire for just one more was like a small fire inside us. Because, you see, I figured that when we'd given up the razor edge of wanting something, we would be old.

* * *

The little mare I bought in Oklahoma had a fancy registered name, but I called her Wiggles because that's what she did best. I kept her at the trainer's barn. She was known as a snowflake Appaloosa with a rump that seemed to have just come out of a snowstorm while the rest of her was the color of a Nutter Butter cookie. With typical Appaloosa eyes that are most like a human's, with white sclera surrounding the eyeball, she always seemed to be giving me the stink eye.

All year I worked hard at learning to ride her. And she worked hard at trying to let me. When it came time to go to the championship, I spent as much time designing my outfit as I had spent on my wedding dress. I ordered custom fringed chaps in tan and a brocade jacket with jewels at my neck. I bought gaudy rhinestone earrings. There was a class in the program, which I studied hard, called Ladies' Western Pleasure. I wasn't sure I could qualify as a lady, and furthermore, I really didn't want to—at least as some people interpret "a lady," i.e., avoiding getting dirty and being excused from taking on hard, troublesome things, as well as an innocence that would never fit with my worldview. Not qualifying as a lady did not rule out being polite and respectful. It was the sort of way "ladies" were thought of as not having gumption, as always having to be protected, as needing to be asked to step out of the room when the complications of life were discussed—those were the things that rubbed me raw. My childhood had more than once tossed off the command to "act like a lady." It was too late now to go back.

I bought myself a saddle with so much silver on it, it was as if my Mississippi grandmother's tea service had been melted down. The week before we were to leave for Oklahoma, I gave Wiggles a hot oil treatment by heating up six bottles of VO5 in a coffeepot and pouring it over her.

I would be in Oklahoma for ten days with Wiggles and her trainer. I worried about leaving Buddy that long. Stella had died by then—heart failure—leaving me the wonderful memory of her enigmatic smile. Without Stella and me, would Buddy run off? Would he go looking for me? Would he hang around the house and barn as usual? Or hit the road? We didn't have a fenced yard. The property was too large for that, and I never liked the idea of a dog pen. Usually I kept Buddy inside with me when I was not at the barn or riding Skip.

I hired a caretaker to come each day to feed him and Skip, but still there was the nagging question as to whether or not he could handle ten days without me before he would go hunting and be run over, or, worse, kidnapped by those who wanted to put a spiked collar on him to show how tough they themselves were. I knew my husband would also look out for him when he was home, but he was spending long, long days in the war against brain tumors.

It was a hot morning in July when I put Wiggles on a trailer headed to the show. The trip would take two days. "Don't let her lie down," I told the cowboy driver. "I want her tired when she gets there." I wanted her not to have enough energy to buck me off or do something risky. She was only four, equal to the age of a human girl of twelve, and you know how those preteen girls can be—dashing at the mall here and there, more interested in snagging a boyfriend and trying on the latest fashions than acting sane.

I flew on a plane to meet her. But when she arrived, she wasn't the least bit tuckered out. In fact, she was wiggling in her stall as if she'd flown out first class with her feet propped up.

My husband came out to see me do my thing. He was by then running marathons. So we were equaling each other in taking on accomplishments that might give us memories in old age. When he saw the way the other women were dressed for their western pleasure classes, he said, "You're never going to win until you get a bigger belt buckle." It was true. Mine was the size of a broach on my Mississippi grandmother's coat. Other riders had belt buckles the size of serving plates, and he bought me one.

On the day I was to ride in my first event, I polished the saddle and Wiggles up so they were both about as shiny as the chrome on a Maserati. The whole time I had to remind myself not to squat while I had on spurs. My husband then went into the stands to watch me ride in on Wiggles. Later he said that when he saw me come jogging in wearing that outrageously gaudy outfit—but definitely looking fine—it was the first time he realized he had married an Arkansas woman.

There were so many of us competing, cowboys lined up at the entrance to the arena like traffic cops to motion us in one at a time. Country music played in the background, some song by Mary Chapin Carpenter about how you could wake up feeling lucky.

The arena was enormous, and it was air-conditioned. When Wiggles hit the cool air, she jumped up and landed in a whole new place, and started trotting.

Someone called out commands on a microphone, but it was all I could do to keep Wiggles halfway aimed at where I wanted to go. She side-swiped one judge and came flat-out toward another so that he ran like a crab to let us miss him. When she and I were back beside the rail, Wiggles stuck her nose in the back end of the horse in front and lifted her own rear end to kick at the one behind. Finally, after we lined up in front of the judges, she set about wiggling so fiercely, I began scratching her over her withers to keep her standing in one spot— except *that* had its own side effect. For it was then that she lifted her head and rolled her upper lip over her nose.

Outside the arena, I got off. I noticed that everyone was giving us a wide berth. In fact, a lot of people were watching us, and all the riders were making their horses walk in big circles away from us. Especially the ones on stallions. And that's when it dawned on me what the real trouble was.

I walked over to the cowboy who had driven Wiggles there and handed him the reins.

"Take her home," I said. "I'm going home too."

I watched him lead Wiggles off. With a menopausal woman on a mare in heat, it was only a matter of time before everybody asked us to leave.

*And I'll never forget
hearing my daughter's
seven-year-old voice
trash-talking before she
even knew what trash-
talking was, protecting me
the best way she could.*

CHAPTER SIXTEEN

The Perfect Gift

Of course I was down in the dumps. I would have to leave and fly home with nothing but a bruised ego to show for my time there. My husband had already flown back to take care of his patients, so I was by myself on the airplane heading back from Oklahoma, sitting beside a seven-year-old boy and his mother. As I stole glances of his perfect self with arms, face, short legs in blue jeans, while listening to the flutelike sound of his voice, it made me think of the day my son was dropped off from a carpool. I was writing in my studio upstairs in the house we lived in before building our home on Blueberry Hill Farm. My son got out of the car and came into the house, then panicked. He didn't think of looking for me upstairs and instead ran, trying to chase the carpool car down the long driveway yelling, "She's not here! I can't find her. Help! Don't leave!" Trotting toward him, I called. "I'm here. I was just upstairs. I'm here." The look on his face was the classic definition of relief and love.

That moment stayed with me all these years as a perfect sweet memory holding the meaning of motherhood as clearly as it can ever be felt. It was matched by the memory of my daughter on the day when I volunteered to be a field trip chaperone. As we walked through the zoo, I overheard a classmate say to my daughter, "Your mama walks funny." My daughter shot back, "Don't talk about my mama!" She said it as well as a three-hundred-pound football player talking trash before a game. "Yo' Mama"— those are universal fighting words. And I'll never forget hearing my daughter's seven-year-old voice trash-talking before she even knew what trash-talking was, protecting me the best way she could.

Now there on the plane flying back from the

botched horse show in Oklahoma, I experienced one of my most life-affirming moments. Just as we were coming in for a landing, the heavens opened up with one of those gully-whopper thunderstorms. Frog stranglers, we Floridians call them. You know the kind: so much lightning, rain, and thunder that I began to wonder if my affairs were enough in order to keep my relatives from squabbling over the piddling stuff I'd leave.

We bounced around for a while, like one of those carnival rides I never had enough guts to buy a ticket for. Then the pilot came on over the loud-speaker and said in his smooth-as-chewing-gum voice that it was way too rough for him to try to set us down here, so he was just going to head on over to Jacksonville and set us down there. A low moan of complaint moved throughout the coach section. Not only did we now face another thirty-minute plane ride, but our relatives or friends who had come to meet us were now standing down there on the ground being told we would be a no-show. The plan was that a bus was being sent to pick us up at the other airport, and then we'd have to ride it all the way back.

The boy beside me, in his jeans, boots, and plaid shirt, had a cowlick over his forehead like a hand of cards. His mother wore shorts and a ruffled blouse. They reminded me of people I had grown up with in the Arkansas cotton belt. More than likely their lives moved to the rhythm of weather and crops or night shifts and overtime. When I asked them who would be waiting for them, I learned that the boy's father had driven fifty miles to be at the airport. Our delay was a real bummer, we agreed. The mother was a good bit distressed. It was then that I witnessed the most amazing exchange.

While the rest of us ducked back into our magazines or went on grumbling about our inconvenience, the boy began telling his mother stories. I don't know what they were about, or where he got them, but looking at his mother's face you would have thought he was telling her the most wonderful and hilarious tales she'd ever heard. She was laughing and watching him as if his every third sentence held the most delicious surprise. More than once, she reached over and punched him on the arm and cried out, "Stop, stop! I can't take it anymore," as if she were being tickled to death. The more she teasingly punched him, the more he talked on.

Throughout our whole ride, even after we were taxiing down the runway into our detoured airport, the boy and his mother continued their exchange. When I got up to get my bag out of the overhead compartment, I glanced down at them. The boy's mother was still listening. I could see that without a doubt the most wondrous light had been lit in that boy's face.

I'm pretty sure it's still there. In fact, I'm pretty convinced that if anything lasts at all, it is this kind of light that is eternal. And it was a privilege to have been there when it was given.

*Buddy felt my need
to be the center of
someone's world, and
he needed someone to
be center of his world.
We were a perfect match.*

CHAPTER SEVENTEEN

I Finally Find the Answer

I came back from riding in the Appaloosa National Championship and wrote down the story that came from that. NPR used it for the opening of the National Cowgirl Museum and Hall of Fame in Fort Worth, Texas, centered on the theme that a dream can be dusted off and squeezed back into life. When the outcome of my dream turned out to be a comic failure, it could then encourage listeners to take their own mess-ups as their share and move on. At the least, my story made it clear that often the story we want to tell is not the best one for us to tell.

But there was more behind the humorous story I told on national radio. For, as soon as I came home, Buddy came to greet me, not in the tail-wagging, tongue-licking mania of most dogs but instead in the matter-of-fact moment of when I, as a mother of teenagers, would come home from a trip somewhere and my kids would clearly be glad but would more or less yell from room to room, "She's back!" Buddy looked at me as if saying too, "I knew you'd come back."

I was still on the trail of trying to answer what exactly Buddy saw in me that I did not see in myself. I didn't find it then. Yet I couldn't quite give up chasing down that answer in some kind of profound understanding. Back when I was in elementary school, I remember being given a test to place me in some class or other. The result I overheard sounded like, "We're just not sure what to do with her."

I took it as a belief that my intelligence was one that simply could not be measured. I know now just what that was—creativity and passion cannot be quantified. When I read somewhere that Picasso had trouble with math because he thought all 7s looked like upside-down noses, I took comfort.

This same wacky thinking kicked in when I decided to write a book about the first successful kidney transplant. You see, I'd known the men who'd accomplished that. And since that medical achievement is considered one of the greatest contributions to humankind in the twentieth century, I wanted to take it on. After all, it's about eliminating suffering. And yet today, it's taken as a matter of course to save a life by the use of a borrowed kidney. So there I was thinking that even though I had made a C in college zoology, I could master the information to explain how the immune system works and impart to the general public the background story of a man-made miracle.

I then applied that confidence to look into recent research on the canine brain. After the year 2000, new scientific findings about dogs began making their way into books for the general public. I was thinking I might finally understand *how* and *why* Buddy and I had leapt the divide across species to form an unbreakable bond. I also still wanted to know *why*, exactly, he had chosen me, what he saw in me that I did not see in myself. I needed a deep, impressive, academic sort of way to explain *us*. In books by Alexandra Horowitz and Gregory Berns, who both studied dogs from a scientist's perspective, there was the answer.

Ms. Horowitz wrote her book when she was the head of the Dog Cognition Lab at Columbia University, and Dr. Berns published his findings in 2013 as a neuroscientist at Emory University. We all know that dogs' noses—like a box of crayons with an endless variety of colors—can detect an enormous number of scents. But their eyes are different too. Human eyes face forward. Our retinae at the back of the eyeballs have *foveae*, which means that we have an abundance of photoreceptors. With so many cells in the center of the retina, we are very good at seeing things right in front of us in high detail, great focus, and strong color. Only primates have foveae, whereas dogs have *area centralis,* which is a central region with fewer receptors. What is directly in front of a dog's face is very visible to him, but not as sharply in focus as what we could see. Thus, a dog doesn't see in detail what is near him until he steps back. Here's the effect: Once a dog opens his eyes to us, he starts gazing at us.[34]

Dogs see us, but the differences in their vision allow them to see things about us that we don't see. In a sense, they are looking straight into our minds. When Dr. Berns studied the MRIs of a few dogs' brains, he saw the area of the brain that houses mirror neurons light up. Mirror neurons are the certain type that activate when an animal moves and sees that movement imitated by another animal. Many researchers suggest that mirror neurons are the brain's source of empathy. In that sense, dogs can read our feelings.[35]

Another book, *Your Dog Is Your Mirror*, by

dog trainer Kevin Behan, echoed those findings in a profound self-awareness. "When I was looking at Illo (my dog) and feeling angry, embarrassed, or ashamed—because in an unscripted moment he would avoid someone's eye or shrink from a stranger's hand—the truth was, he was acting just as I used to act as a little boy. He was me."[36]

So there it was, the scientific answer to what Buddy saw in me that I did not fully see in myself. His longing to own me matched my quiet sorrow in living my days of retired motherhood. It was a jolt realizing that I would no longer be the center of a child's life. Of course motherhood would always be on my CV, but that title is stripped of the sound of a young child's voice calling for me. (And as we all know, there is no greater sound on earth than the sweet, innocent tone of a young child's voice.)

Conclusion: Buddy felt my need to be the center of someone's world, and he needed someone to be the center of his world. We were a perfect match.

Coda

It's said that a coda is a musical section that is distinctive from the main structure, conveying the feeling of a conclusion. So, too, life at my beloved farm changed. To finish out my cowgirl journey, I bought a filly and named her Precious because I thought it'd be funny to give the usual name of a poodle to a thousand-pound animal. Some days, however, she was semiprecious. We were like mother and daughter, often arguing about who was in charge. She was only three, so I hired a trainer from Holland, and then had to give voice commands in a Dutch accent, which was a strange mix with my Arkansas twang.

Skip developed a keratoma, which is a kind of tumor, in his front left hoof. It was surgically removed, yet, in time, he foundered; this was the condition that Secretariat died of. (Skip would like being named in a sentence with Secretariat.) I kept Skip going, though, until he was twenty-eight by strapping on rubber shoes every time he was turned out into the Blueberry Hill Farm pasture.

I lost Buddy after a decade of our sharing most of our days. That's the price of loving a dog. In most cases, we will inevitably outlive them. But I had him for nearly ten years, and despite the pain of his not being with me now, I am a more complete human, a kinder, tougher, more empathetic being. I have what astronauts call in an earthling "enhanced empathy." I have also moved into the season of maturity that comes with reaching a last chapter. I know grief. I know that it is in proportion to the amount of love I felt and gave.

When Buddy developed a cancerous bone in his front leg, I made the decision he would not want to hop around three-legged. There was also the chance the cancer would come back somewhere else. Now I agonize over that decision. Maybe I should have let him live longer, hopping on three legs. If it had been a back leg, I'd have likely made that decision. But a front leg for a dog is a whole other level of a hard life. And I couldn't tolerate his suffering, his crying out whenever he stood up and walked. I let him go.

When the vet I chose to come put him down on Blueberry Hill Farm was giving him the drugs to render him unconscious, Buddy tried to crawl toward me. The vet commented, "He sure has a thing for you."

A thing for me.

Yes, he sure did. And now he is a sweet memory dancing in the sunset when I sit on the porch of Blueberry Hill Farm, aka Gorilla Glue Ranch. I've had three dogs since Buddy. None has given me the same feeling as Buddy. We were like the sound of a piano's middle C and a G being played together: a perfect chord. As he and I connected across the space of different species, I became like that astronaut Ron Garan swinging on the Space Station's Canadarm2 arm with Buddy pushing it in a wide arc. I look at the Earth and see life differently. I know that I can receive love and give it in equal measure, no questions asked. In the whole scope of things, that's no small achievement.

In Marjorie Kinnan Rawlings's memoir *Cross Creek,* she writes about the ten years she lived at the Creek tending an orange grove to support her while she wrote *The Yearling,* which would become one of the greatest novels in American literature. She described one day with majestic prose: "The universe and the world inside it breathed the same breath. This was the cosmic life, with suns and moons to make it lovely. It was important only to keep close enough to the pulse to feel its rhythm, to be comforted by its steadiness, to know that Life

is vital, and one's own minute living a torn frag-
ment of the larger cloth."[37]

As for my own prose, a critic once said my
writing tends to get flowery. True, when something
uncorks my love, the words gush out. This time I'll
throw in a few mosquitoes to keep it level. For when
I sit on the porch of my beloved farm to watch the
summer sun set on the other side of the pasture, I
seem to hear the opening notes of "Ol' Man River"
as a low humming. At eight o'clock I peek from
behind one of the house columns, which is the only
way my eyes will let me look directly at what seems
like a swollen egg yolk balancing on the horizon.
The intensity of the sun's light is as straight-on as a
rap singer doing an in-your-face rhyme.

At 8:10 it is as if a peach has exploded in
a hallelujah of juice, leaving a layer of blueberry
grayness. The sun slips away as if it were a diva
ducking behind a curtain, and I feel as if I am in a
grand cathedral.

The poet John Greenleaf Whittier wrote that beauty seen is never lost, that all God's colors last. Oscar Wilde said that nobody of any real culture ever talks about the beauty of sunsets, that sunsets are quite old-fashioned and to admire them is a distinct sign of provincialism of temperament. He also added that, on the other hand, they go on.

At the edge of the porch, a bullfrog croaks, sounding like someone banging on a hollow pipe. Surrounded by the sounds of July flies and crickets, while smelling the honey-sweetness of jasmine, I am the object of a mosquito's desire, buzzing around, picking out the tastiest part of me to land on. While I know that I am living on a planet circling the sun at one hundred thousand miles an hour, hurling through our galaxy of the Milky Way, it's hard to comprehend or even imagine that. When the sun is totally gone, I'm tempted to hum a few bars of a lullaby, for the habits of mothers tend to go on too.

Understanding the concept of home only

comes around a few times in a lifetime. Buddy made me know that. All those years I spent with him are now like images shimmering under water. Among my most appreciative thoughts of him, though, is that he never threw a clinker in my boast of being a good kisser.

Continuing the Conversation

Before its publication, early readers of this book asked for a picture of Skip. This also gives me a chance to say a few more things, because without you as readers, we writers would be singing in the dark. It is *you* who are the connective tissue of our nation and world, passing on stories. I hope that you enjoyed this true slice of my life as I lived it with the chance you will feel peace, hope, and comfort from its pages. And if not, please donate this book to a thrift shop. In any case, thank you! Being born with words in my fingers itching to be written down or pecked out on a keyboard can make one hard to live with. So another hardy thanks to my family who have learned to live with this grown-old kindergarten dictator.

I realize that I have tinkered with the traditional genre of memoir. Telling pretty much my whole life around the story of a dog means I have poured my memories onto those I have loved. I highly recommend this method. Also, since I have lived through a lot of history, I have been told that I used some references that leave my reader behind. To fill in this hole, I add: the *Beloved Community* is formed by those who think we should strive for a world absent of poverty and hunger, and to end hate. The requirement for membership is to practice loving our neighbors— even when they aren't like those in *Mister Rogers' Neighborhood* or in an episode of *Friends*.

Special thanks to Becky Nesbitt for the honor she gave me of having this book be among her first releases in her new Resolve Books imprint. To Kia Harris, thanks for getting it all done; to Amanda Bauch for making it smooth; to Billie Brownell for polishing it all up; and to Carisa Hayes, who made sure almost everyone in the world would know about its appearance on publication day.

To America's most revered historian of our founding history, Gordon Wood, who kindly answered the phone when I called asking how the Jefferson–Adams broken friendship is relevant to us today—you are among the kindest people I've known. Professor Wood made me know that until we read history, we live with delusions. So now I keep one of his big books on my bedside table so if I die in the night, it'll make me look good.

As for the revered physicist Carlo Rovelli, when I emailed him to see if he would be OK with my quoting from his book, *Seven Brief Lessons on Physics*, I didn't really expect him to answer. You know how emails go—easy to dismiss. But he wrote back right away and asked to see a PDF of the manuscript. After he read the pages that referred to his work, he sent back a smiling emoji. The value of emojis is that they need no translation. Thank you,

Mr. Rovelli, you are among the most warmhearted people on the planet.

With an appreciative nod to my college friends Priscilla and Billy Sumrall, who taught me that you can laugh through anything, even the dark stuff, if you wait long enough to find the comic angle. When they told me they named their daughter after me, I thought, *Gosh! They're brave!* Indeed, their child named Shelley has turned out to have the same obsessive passion for paint and canvas as I have for words and books.

Now, as promised, here's Skip and me aiming for a blue ribbon in a horse show before I understood that a honking big belt buckle can help, plus make your waist look small before you lose your waist. As for another of my heroes, remember this: Norman Cousins wrote that humor is more than a source of laughter and good feelings: "It is a way of responding to life. It is a way of reaching other human beings and creating attachments and understandings difficult to achieve in any other way."[38] Even that old sourpuss Nietzsche said, "The most acutely suffering animal on earth invented laughter."[39]

Keep laughing. I love you.

Shelley Mickle, February 2025

Recipes

I won't beat around the bush here: I hate to cook. All that standing up is hard for me, and it takes time. I'd much rather be working on a novel. And contrary to what some think, writing consumes an immense amount of time. It's not just a matter of sitting down at the kitchen table after the dishes are done and beating out words on a keyboard or by longhand. Go ahead and weep for me.

But since cooking is definitely an act of love—and I love my family to an immeasurable degree—I did conquer some recipes. Every day about 6 p.m., I would shovel a meal onto the table, carefully planned according to the nutritional color wheel: a green vegetable, something yellow or starchy, a meat, and often a dessert.

This leads me to a confession, and in "Godfather" talk, if you tell anyone, I'll have to kill you. You see, in the arsenic hour when my toddlers were too exhausted to eat, I'd put a dollop of ice cream on their plates, which melted into the green beans and then into the cooked squash until they lapped up the river of goodness while I cautioned: "Don't breathe a word of what your mama just did."

Exhausted Neurosurgical Residents' Pork Chops

Once when my husband was training in neuro-surgery, he brought home a fellow resident for dinner. I cooked a whole package of eight pork chops, thinking I'd have leftovers so as not to have to cook the next day. But they ate them all! Dr. Gordon McComb, if you still remember this supper in the little rented farmhouse on Lincoln Road, here's the inside story of how I rustled up the grub.

- Get a rolling pen and beat the hell out of the chops.

- Dredge them in flour.

- Slap them in a skillet with a little oil and pray.

- Turn them over once until they are one degree from burned.

- Pour in a little water; clap on a lid so the skillet steams.

Dogs But Not Real Dogs

I can cook a hot dog like nobody's business. I came up with this on my own. But for fun, please credit Julia Child. I think she'd laugh.

- Split the dog or wienie, whichever nomenclature you prefer.

- Mash it hard on a hot cast-iron skillet until it curls.

- Slice the bun and mash it down onto the hot skillet until it's thinking about coming up toasted.

- Put the dog on the bun with mustard, relish, catsup, chili, slaw, or any other heaven-sent condiment, and wolf it down. There are no adjectives to describe the sound that you will utter after the first bite.

Catch It on Fire

My hairdresser and I exchange recipes while he's doing my hair. I like to tell him something I've come up with on my own. But he's a really good cook, so I mostly entertain him. Once while he was giving me a curl-up-and-dye job, I told him about my relationship with the fancy grill I'd bought. When I could finally light it without losing my eyebrows, I shared how I cooked this larrupin' good chicken.

- Get the grill really hot, about 500 degrees
- Paint skinless chicken breasts with olive oil and put them on the grill, wishing them the best.
- When they catch on fire, turn the grill off, put down the hood, and let the breasts sweat it out.

After trying this, my hairdresser encouraged me to write a cookbook titled *Catch It on Fire! !*

How to Cheat
at Thanksgiving Dinner

We Southerners know that Thanksgiving dinner is the Olympics of cooking. I once walked into the kitchen on Thanksgiving Day and saw my mother crying. Of course, everybody else was sitting in Naugahyde recliners watching football games or telling whoppers, oblivious to my mother's meltdown. When I asked what was wrong, she said in a trembling voice, "I can't get my turkey gravy to thicken." That's every Southern cook's nightmare. But my dear hairdresser, who helps me now get through Thanksgiving cooking, told me the cure. (Thanks, Jim Lee.)

- Open one of those packets of chicken gravy that you mix with water.

- Throw in a few packets of turkey gravy if you want to feel honest.

- Add a sliced boiled egg.

- Add bits of the cooked turkey liver.

- Add some cooked turkey juice.

- Put in fresh mushrooms sautéed in butter.

- Add a handful of cut-up parsley.

No one can suspect that your turkey gravy is not made from turkey drippings, and you have not only saved oodles of time but also averted a public nervous breakdown. (We're all allowed several nervous breakdowns; just avoid having them in public. In any case, be sure to wear nice perfume and nail polish. A well-groomed woman will never be mistaken for being cold-out crazy.)

Lasagna to Make a Man Weak in the Knees

- Start with lots of ground beef, browned.

- Chop in an onion.

- Shake in some salt unless he has high blood pressure; in that case, rely on Mrs. Dash.

- Throw in a can of tomato sauce and tomato paste, one egg, some small curd cottage cheese, oregano, basil, and garlic powder.

- Put the boiled lasagna noodles and the whole shebang together—you know how to do this— there's not a woman alive who does not know the effect of lasagna on a man, which is second only to his love for a ribeye.

- If your man is a vegetarian (God love him), then substitute the meat with spinach mixed with ricotta and eggs.

- Top with a little sauce and mozzarella cheese.

- Cook in the oven. And if you're really desperate for his attention, serve it naked.

Utterly Deadly
Sweet Potato Pie

I often cook from Marjorie Rawlings's cookbook. At the same time she was writing a novel that is an American masterpiece, she was also cooking and having dinner guests such as Robert Frost. She could never get Hemingway to come to dinner at Cross Creek, but she met him at a restaurant near St. Augustine. She called cooking her one vanity. At her home at Cross Creek, she had to cook on a woodburning stove. This is the proof that a woman with literary aspirations does not have to eschew cooking from the fear it will make her seem like a fluff-butt.

Marjorie's sweet potato pie is to die for. Since I

like to avoid recipes with sugar, I was thrilled to see that Marjorie's pie substitutes honey. Here's my version.

- Get about 4 sweet potatoes.

- Bake or microwave them.

- Split them open and spoon out the golden sweet potato, which always reminds me of what my husband said when I told him NPR had just invited me to be a commentator. He lamented, "But you're not a common tater; you're a sweet 'tator.'"

- Use my trick if you're brave: put the cooked potato in a blender.

- Add 2 eggs, a cup of milk, ½ cup of honey, some cinnamon, and the juice squeezed from one whole orange.

- Turn on the blender. When all the ingredients are whipped together, pour the mixture into one of those prepared pie pastries and cook in the oven at a high temperature for about 10 minutes to set the liquid, then bake for a long time at about 350 degrees until you can stick a knife in, and it comes out clean.

Be sure to put the lid on the blender before you turn it on. Once while everyone waited at the table for my pie to be served hot, I was too busy to notice I had not put the top on the blender. When I sat down at the table and smiled sweetly, I had to pick hunks of sweet potato out of my hair.

If you serve Marjorie's Sweet Potato Pie warm straight from the oven with a dollop of whipped cream, you're likely to hear your family singsong, "My, my!" Simply lost for words—but in a good way. When Marjorie served it, she always said she could hear angels sing.

Homeroom Mother's Eggs

When my kids were young, I volunteered to be the homeroom mother. Other mothers were busy being lawyers or doctors, teachers, therapists, or something essential like that. Being a writer who worked at home didn't seem to be a good reason not to volunteer.

However, I was an awful homeroom mother. Instead of baking the holiday cupcakes, I bought them at the grocery and sped them to the school—usually while gnawing over a sentence or chapter I'd been writing that morning.

One day when my son was in first grade, I was taking him to school while speeding the cupcakes for a Halloween Party. I heard a siren.

I rarely look in the rearview mirror. But when this policeman began blinking his blue lights, I finally caught on that he really was after me. I pulled over.

I could see my son's eyes in the rearview mirror, looking horrified.

When the police officer came close, I rolled down the window and handed him a cupcake. I guess that cupcake could really have been seen as a bribe. But the policeman turned down the cupcake and wrote a speeding ticket.

Later I learned that at Show-and-Tell, my son announced that this would his last day at school, for tomorrow he was going to prison with his mother.

However, I redeemed myself at the holiday party.

This was the day when all the kids and their parents were coming for breakfast. I was going to cook fifty eggs in two batches. I wore a fancy apron. I fixed my hair. I wore poinsettia-red lipstick. When word got out that I was in the school kitchen scrambling fifty eggs, some parents came to watch.

I didn't know that some people consider scrambling eggs to be a dangerous business. The challenge is to scramble them without them drying out, becoming hard, or lying on a plate like a glob of small, round yellow things resembling a clump of fish eggs.

- Put butter in a big skillet.
- Crack in half the eggs so you'll be making two batches to feed fifty people.
- Break the yellows with a spatula.
- Pour in some liquid egg mixture.
- Add pieces of yellow American cheese.
- Use the spatula like the conductor of the London Symphony. *Don't* stir the eggs—fold them. Imagine you're making a cloud, the looping kind that floats in the sky seemingly by magic. Fold, fold. This is the crucial part. Cook over low medium heat. This takes a while.

While you are doing this, tell jokes. That day while the parents watched, I kept them clean, such as: A chicken and a pig were walking down the road. They saw a sign:

EGG AND HAM BREAKFAST FOR A WORTHY CAUSE.

The chicken said, "Let's stop and help."

The pig shook his head. "For you it means an egg or two, but for me, it's a commitment."

That day, I learned something profound: I have a major talent for scrambling eggs. The truth is, I simply winged it, hoping not to embarrass my son. But those scrambled eggs turned out to be . . . well, super delicious. So even today, some of those parents who have grown old as I have will come up to me and say, "Would you kindly give me that recipe for scrambled eggs you made for the party when our kids were in first grade?

Can I get a patent?

Sources

Donald M. Borchert, ed., *The Encyclopedia of Philosophy* Vol. 3 (Thomson Gale, 2006).

Behan, Kevin, *Your Dog Is Your Mirror* (New World Library, 2011).

Berns, Gregory, *How Dogs Love Us* (New Harvest, 2013).

Cousins, Norman, *Head First: The Biology of Hope* (Dutton, 1989).

Ellis, Joseph, *American Sphinx* (Vintage, 1998).

Fried, Stephan, *RUSH* (Crown, 2018).

Horowitz, Alexandra, *Inside of a Dog* (Scribner's, 2010).

Jennison, Keith W., *The Humorous Mr. Lincoln: A Profile in Wit, Courage, and Compassion with an Introduction by Norman Cousins* (Woodstock, 1988).

McCullough, David, *John Adams* (Simon & Schuster, 2001).

Meacham, Jon, *Thomas Jefferson, The Art of Power* (Random House, 2013).

Perkins, John, *Shapeshifting: Shamanic Techniques for Global and Personal Transformation* (Destiny Books, 1997).

Randall, Henry, *The Life of Thomas Jefferson* (Lippincott & Co., 1865).

Rawlings, Marjorie Kinnan, *Cross Creek* (Simon & Schuster, 1996).

Rawlings, Marjorie Kinnan, *The Yearling* (reprint edition, Aladdin, 2001).

Rovelli, Carlo, *Seven Brief Lessons on Physics* (Riverhead, 2016); and "Carlo Rovelli: Seven Brief Lessons on Physics," World Book Club, podcast, https://podcasts.apple.com/us/podcast/carlo-rovelli-seven-brief-lessons-on-physics/id263658343?i=1000643844561.

Rydell, Mark, dir., *The Reivers* (National General Pictures, 1969).

Schiff, Stacy, *The Revolutionary: Samuel Adams* (Little, Brown and Company, 2022).

Unger, Harlow Giles, *Benjamin Rush* (Da Capo Press, 2018).

Welty, Eudora, *One Time, One Place: Mississippi in the Depression* (University Press of Mississippi, 1971).

White, Frank, *The Overview Effect, Space Exploration and Human Evolution*, 4th Ed. (Multiverse, 2021).

You can contact Shelley at www. Shelleymickle.com

Notes

1. Paul Edwards, Editor in Chief, *The Encyclopedia of Philosophy* (Pearson College Div., 1967), 91–93.

2. Norman Cousins, *Head First: The Biology of Hope and the Healing Power of the Human Spirit* (Dutton, 1989), 133.

3. Keith W. Jennison, *The Humorous Mr. Lincoln* (Woodstock, 1988), 20.

4. Jennison, *The Humorous Mr. Lincoln*, 38.

5. John Perkins, *Shapeshifting* (Destiny Books, 1997), 2–4.

6. Perkins, *Shapeshifting*, 3.

7. Marjorie Rawlings, *The Yearling* (Aladdin, 2001 reprint edition), 426.

8. Frank White, *The Overview Effect, Space Exploration and Human Evolution*, 4th ed. (Multiverse, 2021), 37.

9. White, *The Overview Effect*, 39.

10. White, 39.

11. White, 40.

12. White, 37.

13. White, 391.

14. White, xvi.

15. White, xv.

16. White, 188.

17. White,190.

18. White, xx.

19. White, xvii.

20. White, 192.

21. Joseph Ellis, *American Sphinx* (Vintage, 1998), 65.

22. Henry Randall, *The Life of Thomas Jefferson, Vol.1* (Lippincott & Co., 1865), 384.

23. Stephen Fried, *RUSH* (Crown, 2018), 137.

24. David McCullough, *John Adams* (Simon & Schuster, 2001), 640.

25. McCullough, *John Adams*, 106.

26. McCullough, 107.

27. Stacy Schiff, *The Revolutionary: Samuel Adams* (Little, Brown and Company, 2022), 99.

28. Carlo Rovelli, *Seven Brief Lessons on Physics* (Riverhead, 2016), 78.

29. Rovelli, *Seven Brief Lessons on Physics*, 78.

30. Rovelli, *Seven Brief Lessons on Physics*, 78.

31. Mark Rydell, dir, *The Reivers*, National General Pictures, 1969; adapted from William Faulkner, *The Reivers* (Random House, 1962).

32. Encyclopedia Britannica, T4 Program.

Notes

33. Eudora Welty, *One Time, One Place* (University Press of Mississippi, 1971), frontispiece.

34. Alexandra Horowitz, *Inside of a Dog* (Scribner's, 2010), 137.

35. Gregory Berns, *How Dogs Love Us* (New Harvest, 2013), 191.

36. Kevin Behan, *Your Dog Is Your Mirror* (New World Library, 2011), 295.

37. Marjorie Kinnan Rawlings, *Cross Creek* (Simon & Schuster, 1996), 39.

38. Keith W. Jennison, *The Humorous Mr. Lincoln: A Profile in Wit, Courage, and Compassion* (Woodstock, 1988), introduction.

39. Norman Cousins, *Head First* (Dutton, 1989), 125.